Endeavor®

8 ------- Teacher's Guide

New Readers Press®
ProLiteracy's publishing division

Endeavor® 8: Teacher's Guide
ISBN 978-1-56420-876-7

Copyright © 2009 New Readers Press
New Readers Press
ProLiteracy's Publishing Division
104 Marcellus Street, Syracuse, New York 13204
www.newreaderspress.com

Printed in the United States of America
19

Proceeds from the sale of New Readers Press materials support professional
development, training, and technical assistance programs of ProLiteracy
that benefit local literacy programs in the U.S. and around the globe.

Contributing Author: Vista Resources, Inc.
Developmental Editors: Ellen Northcott, Donna Townsend
Creative Director: Andrea Woodbury
Production Specialist: Maryellen Casey

Contents

Strategies for Success with *Endeavor*

Tips for Planning Instruction

There are a number of strategies that you can implement to maximize the effectiveness of *Endeavor's* lesson plans. First, always prepare your lessons before class. This includes reading and practicing the text of the story, selecting activities, and preparing materials. Although the *Endeavor* Teacher's Guide is intended to provide ideas and guidance, it is not meant as a script. Use the explanations in the Teacher's Guide to help you develop explanations in your own words. Additionally, modify the questions, examples, and activities to suit the needs of your students. If, for example, some students need more time to complete an element in the lesson, determine which activities you can omit or shortcut in order for students to have the time they need to be successful. Remember, the objective is for students to feel satisfaction as they become aware of their gains in building reading, writing, and other language skills.

Tips for Implementing Instruction

Students should be clear about what is expected of them. Therefore, inform students of the learning goals and outcomes before beginning a lesson. This Teacher's Guide provides learning objectives on the first page of notes for each lesson. Students should also be clear about how they will perform the tasks required of them. It is imperative, therefore, that you model every new skill, and model skills again if your students have not practiced them in a while. For example, model a sentence that uses a new vocabulary word correctly and in a meaningful context, and then work with students to explain what made your sentence effective. This kind of explicit skill modeling will make your expectations clear to your students. Students will begin to internalize what constitutes a complete answer or a meaningful interaction with a text.

In addition to modeling skills, you will also want to model strategies. Create your own Think About Its to complement those incorporated in the student book. Modeling how you think as you read will provide students with concrete examples of the ways that they should be interacting with text. If you realize that your students have never taken notes as they read, model notetaking. Use a text photocopied onto an overhead transparency and demonstrate how you highlight relevant passages or take notes on the side of the text. The more specific you are and the more examples you give of the various skills and strategies, the clearer the understanding will be in students' minds. Use of the active reading strategies should become second nature to students. This will occur with repetition, so remind them to use strategies that they have already learned.

Fluency and vocabulary development are important components of your students' reading growth. Therefore, you and your students should read aloud whenever possible. Not only will students get to listen to your fluent model and practice their own oral fluency, but students' reading will provide an opportunity for you to do informal assessments. Similarly, the Vocabulary Knowledge Rating Chart (Master 9) can help you to assess your students' facility with words and can inform your vocabulary instruction. If, for instance, most of your students indicate that they fully understand the word *bruised*, but the word *permeated* is unfamiliar, spend your instructional time on the unfamiliar word. Additionally, spend more time on the words that students are likely to encounter in a variety of texts—the key vocabulary words—rather than specialized vocabulary. There are activities and suggestions throughout the Teacher's Guide to assist you in your explanations and planning.

Tips for Maximizing Students as Resources

The life experience of adult learners is invaluable, so make sure that you are bringing students' prior knowledge into every aspect of your teaching. Make your examples relevant to students' experience, and allow them to draw connections between what they are learning and what they already know. The stories and articles in *Endeavor* were selected because they are likely in some way to relate to students' life experiences and concerns. Find those connections, and make them clear to students.

In addition to utilizing students' prior knowledge in your lessons, use students as resources for themselves and one another. The Revising and Editing Checklist (Master 11) is provided as a tool for students. They can check and improve their own and their peers' work using very specific criteria. As always, model the use of the Revising and Editing Checklist, and give students ample opportunity to practice with it. Also, have students use the Writing Rubric (Master 10) to evaluate their completed pieces against measures of ideas, organization, voice, and conventions. Compare your evaluations with theirs as part of writing conferences. These strategies for self- and peer-evaluation do not preclude the need for teacher assessment, but they do give students another set of eyes as they review their own work. The Revising and Editing Checklist and the Writing Rubric allow students to work with and eventually internalize criteria for an acceptable piece of writing.

Assessment is the key to determining if your instruction has been successful and if your students are progressing. You should be using periodic formal assessments, such as the TABE (Tests of Adult Basic Education) or another instrument, to track your students' progress. Informal assessments are important as well, particularly when it comes to modifying your instruction from lesson to lesson. Informal assessments include checklists of skills, over-the-shoulder analyses of students' reading, and your evaluations of students' class work. Although *Endeavor* provides rich resources in terms of texts, activities, strategies, and pedagogy, ultimately it is you, the teacher, who is most important to your students' success. It is your preparation, modeling, and evaluation that will ensure that your students are growing as learners, readers, and writers. We welcome you and wish you luck as you embark on this *Endeavor*.

Suggestions for Developing Vocabulary

Key Vocabulary

The key vocabulary words have been chosen because they are likely to be entirely unfamiliar or somewhat unfamiliar to many students. By working with these words before students begin reading, you are giving students additional keys with which to unlock the meaning of the text. The more they know before reading, the more they are likely to take with them from the reading.

In addition to helping students comprehend a particular text, vocabulary study will provide students with new words to add to their working vocabularies. As their vocabularies grow, they will be able to read increasingly more complex texts. They will also be able to express themselves in a more sophisticated manner in their writing and speaking.

Side-Column Vocabulary

Vocabulary words can be broken down into three tiers. Tier 1 words are the most basic words. These words (like *removed*, *rude*, and *attitude*) do not need to be taught, because they are already part of students' vocabularies. Tier 2 words (like *lethargic*, *sauntered*, and *surreptitiously*) are found in more sophisticated texts and across a variety of domains. These are the kinds of words that have been selected as key vocabulary words.

Tier 3 words (like *bistro*, *cutlery*, and *entrees*) are specialized vocabulary. These words appear infrequently in texts and generally apply only to specific domains. These are the kinds of words that have been selected as side-column vocabulary. Although it will be useful to teach these words in the context of the particular text you are reading, they are not likely to appear frequently or in a variety of texts. Therefore, *Endeavor* focuses more on direct instruction and practice of Tier 2 words than it does on Tier 3 words.

How to Use the Vocabulary Knowledge Rating Chart

The Vocabulary Knowledge Rating Chart (Master 9) is a quick tool for determining students' prior knowledge of each of the vocabulary words. Not only will it help students focus on each of the words, but it will give you a sense of the words on which you will want to concentrate instruction.

Model the use of the Vocabulary Knowledge Rating Chart when you first introduce it. Once students are familiar with the chart, however, they should be able to use it on subsequent sets of words quickly and without extensive instruction.

Tips for Teaching Vocabulary

- The key to learning vocabulary is practice. Each lesson guide includes a number of different strategies for vocabulary practice. Provide as many opportunities as possible for students to interact with and practice the new words.

- Be sure to reframe students' sentences if they are using words incorrectly, and provide additional examples and explanations if necessary. If students learn vocabulary words incorrectly, they will use them incorrectly in the future.

- Use challenging vocabulary when you are talking to your students. Your modeling will help them use words in appropriate contexts, and the unfamiliar words you use will encourage students to explore vocabulary beyond what is being explicitly taught.

- Encourage students to use their new vocabulary words in their everyday lives, and invite them to share anecdotes of when they use the words or encounter the words in conversations or in the media.

Suggestions for Keeping Personal Dictionaries

Personal dictionaries are meant both as spelling aids and as places to record and explore new vocabulary words. For maximum benefit, personal dictionaries should be user-friendly.

A personal dictionary can be created from a notebook or from paper stapled or bound together. It should be its own entity rather than part of another notebook. This will make it more easily accessible and portable as students move through various levels of Endeavor. The personal dictionary should be organized alphabetically and have at least four full pages for each letter, perhaps fewer for the less frequently used letters.

Since vocabulary words are best internalized when they are used often, it is important that personal dictionaries be interactive. Students should enter new words they encounter from their experience and from the texts and other print material they are reading. Ask them to include a clear definition and part of speech along with sentences, examples, sketches, or other means for them to internalize a full, clear meaning of the term. Students should have a voice in deciding what to include in an entry.

Plan frequent activities that require students to return to the words they have recorded. Have students find a "k" word and share it with a neighbor; dramatize a "p" word and have the class guess it; sketch a simple drawing of a word; or write a sentence, correctly using at least three of their vocabulary words. If students simply enter the words and never return to them, the benefit of the personal dictionary will be minimal.

Inside the front and back covers of the personal dictionary, have students record words that are particularly challenging for them to spell. This will limit the number of times they need to search for those words in a large dictionary. It also gives the teacher a place to record words that students are consistently misspelling in their writing. Finally, it ensures that the personal dictionary is being utilized often, as it will be on students' desks as they are writing.

Suggestions for Writing Portfolios

A writing portfolio is intended to hold student work so that the student, teacher, or observer can see how the student has developed as a writer. A portfolio can be a file folder, a box, or a large envelope. Ask each student to create his or her own portfolio. Portfolios can include any writing that the student has done. If the class is producing a lot of work, you will want to pick and choose items for the portfolio so that it doesn't become unmanageable and unusable. Encourage students to include pieces that they are particularly proud of. The goal is to have the contents organized and accessible.

By reviewing their portfolios, students, and particularly adult students, will have the opportunity to evaluate their own work and growth. They will also have access to the teacher's observations and evaluations of their work. Moreover, portfolios might include copies of the Writing Rubric (Master 10) which students can use to evaluate and comment on their own work. Self-evaluations of final drafts of writing can be modeled by the teacher and done often.

Writing portfolios should be interactive rather than stored out of reach. Students use them to review their work and note their progress. In addition, students should have the opportunity to return to a piece they have written, work to improve it, and then publish it in a creative way. By continuing to interact with their writing and evaluating their own progress, students will remain motivated to improve their writing.

Developing Fluency

Fluency is a reader's ability to recognize words automatically and accurately and to read aloud with appropriate expression. The expression is called *prosody*, and it includes intonation, stress, rate, rhythm, and phrasing. Prosody is important to a reader's understanding of the text. Students must comprehend what they are reading in addition to reading quickly and accurately; therefore, teachers must effectively model and teach prosody. And students need repetition in order to develop fluency.

Although the teacher is an important model of fluent reading, the teacher cannot work individually with every student at the same time. Also, in any group of readers, there are likely to be some differences in students' ability to read orally. Therefore, strategies have been developed to help classrooms of readers at different levels to work on fluency simultaneously. These strategies usually include modeling and repetition.

Fluency in *Endeavor*

Endeavor supports you as you work with your students to improve their fluency. Each lesson in the Teacher's Guide provides strategies you can use to practice fluency. With any of the texts, you may wish to use other strategies in addition to those described in the lesson.

Strategies

Echo Reading—With Echo Reading, students imitate fluent reading modeled by the teacher. The teacher reads aloud, and the students are the echo. Depending upon the level of the readers in your class, you will break the

text into phrases or full sentences. Read the phrase or sentence aloud, paying careful attention to your accuracy and prosody. Then have the class repeat the phrase or sentence, also paying careful attention to accuracy and prosody. Continue reading aloud and having the class echo you for the rest of the passage. Be sure to break the text at logical points in order to maintain the meaning of the text.

Choral Reading—Choral Reading involves students reading aloud together, like a chorus. The teacher begins by reading the chosen passage aloud, concentrating on accuracy and prosody. Then students read the same passage aloud in groups ranging from three students to the whole class reading together. In order to set and maintain the pace, the teacher reads aloud with the students. Choral Reading allows readers the opportunity to practice fluency in a situation where they are supported by other readers.

Paired Repeated Reading—Paired Repeated Reading involves students working with one another—rather than one-on-one with the teacher—in order to improve their fluency. Students work in pairs, and each partner selects a passage to read aloud. Students begin by reading their passages silently. Then partners take turns being the reader or listener. Readers read their passages aloud three times. After the first reading, the listener does not provide feedback. After the second and third readings, the listener provides feedback to the reader.

Be sure to explain and model for students how to give one another constructive feedback. Model directly for students, using a volunteer reader. Tell students that comments such as, "I didn't know from your reading that this sentence was a question" or "I could understand you better if you slowed down and read louder" are more helpful than "Good job." Do a *fishbowl* exercise where the class observes a pair of readers and the class gives feedback on the pairs' feedback to one another. Once students are clear on how to give each other feedback, you will not have to repeat the modeling or fishbowl.

Reading to the Teacher—With small numbers of students in a class, it is possible to give regular attention on fluency to individual students. This gives you a clear sense of each student's strengths and weaknesses. Have students choose passages. Give them an opportunity to review them before they read them aloud to you. Give specific and constructive feedback on accuracy and prosody immediately after the reading. You can also use Echo Reading one-on-one to give students the opportunity for repetition.

Popcorn Reading—With popcorn reading, students take turns reading aloud. Students do not know who is going to be reading next, just as you do not know which kernel of corn will pop next. One student reads a sentence, a few sentences, or a paragraph. Then, he or she says "Popcorn, . . ." and calls another student's name. That student reads part of the passage and then *popcorns* someone else. Students stay on their toes, because they do not know who will be reading next.

Performance Reading—Many students enjoy working in pairs or small groups to dramatize the text they are reading. This strategy works well with texts that include a lot of dialogue. Assign students different roles, and have them practice the dialogue for their characters so that they are able to read their parts fluently and with expression from the text. Then have students perform for the class.

Fluency Tips for the Teacher
- Read and prepare the text before coming to class. It is easier to model fluency if you are already familiar with the text.
- Make sure students are familiar with the text before they begin to work on fluency. If students have already worked with the vocabulary and content of

the text, they will struggle less with pronunciation and phrasing.

- You can use different fluency strategies with the same text. On one day, you might choose to use Echo Reading with a particular story; the next day, you might choose a passage from the same story and do Choral Reading. Remember that repetition is one of the keys to enhancing fluency.
- When pairing students, split the class into two groups according to reading ability. Have the top student of your more able readers work with the top student of your less able readers (conversely, have the low student of your best readers work with the lowest student of your lowest readers.) This may minimize frustration while still providing readers with support.

Keeping Track of Students' Progress
You will want to keep track of your students' reading progress. You can do this by informally recording each individual student's reading accuracy.

- Begin by choosing an unfamiliar passage of about 200 words in length that is at the student's reading level (perhaps from the next lesson in his or her student book or from the student books above or below that level.) Have the student read the passage aloud to you.
- On a separate copy of the same text, put a check mark over each word that is properly read. Each time a reader substitutes, omits, or inserts a word, count it as an error. If the student corrects herself, do not count those words as errors.
- Tally the errors and determine the percentage of words that were accurately read.
- Record a student's reading accuracy every few weeks in order to track progress.

Note: Running Records can be used to do a more thorough analysis of a student's reading and enable you to address individual challenges. You can go online to find explanations and examples of Running Records.

Staying Fit and Healthy

Lesson Overview: (PAGE 5)

Theme

Have students read the lesson title on page 5 and tell them that the title introduces the lesson theme, Health. Have students make personal connections, telling what they do to stay healthy, particularly what kinds of exercise they do. Ask them if they know anyone personally or a celebrity who has used steroids or performance-enhancing drugs.

Learning objectives

Be sure students understand the outcome of each of the learning goals.

- *Learn about weight lifting and steroid use.* Point out that the story is fiction. The issues in the story are written to provoke a discussion. The issues are real and based on facts.
- *Make inferences about what you read.*
- *Master the key vocabulary used in the story.*
- *Write a letter to the editor about steroid use.*

Preteach the vocabulary. (PAGE 5)

Read the key vocabulary words and their definitions to the students. Tell them that they will recognize all these words in the story.

- Distribute the Vocabulary Knowledge Rating Chart (Master 9) and have students individually rate each of the key vocabulary words.
- Preview particularly challenging words with students by listing each one on the board, modeling its use in a sentence, and having two or three students use the word in original sentences. Reframe student sentences that do not use the new words correctly.

You may wish to offer a mini-lesson on adverbs as students read the respective parts of speech with the definitions of the vocabulary words. [See page 42 of this book for a mini-lesson on adverbs. Use Master 7 or 8 to give students practice in recognizing adverbs.]

Before You Read (PAGE 6)

Explain that good readers know when they don't understand an element in a story's plot, and they take steps to increase understanding. Point out that good readers focus on the reading, putting questions in the margin where they find things they do not understand. After marking a confusing passage, a good reader forms questions and then rereads to find the answers. Explain that context clues and a dictionary can help with confusing words. Rereading will also help with confusion about an element in the story's plot.

As students begin to write answers to the questions for each element on page 6, have them read the respective Think About Its.

Use what you know. Use the Think About It to elicit discussion about people or athletes students know or have heard of who use steroids. Do they know why athletes choose to use steroids? Do they believe that steroids enhance performance? Some students may not have had any previous exposure to steroids. In that case, tell students that the story will help to create background knowledge for the next time they encounter this topic.

Visualize while you read. Have students read the first paragraph and then discuss with a partner what they think Tim looks like. Have them read the Think About It. Have students compare their descriptions to the impression in the Think About It. Although their thoughts, reactions, and reflections are not likely to mirror the Think About Its exactly, it is likely that they will be similar.

Reading the Story (PAGES 7–9)

Emphasize to students that they will read to learn whether Tim will start taking steroids. If so, what will the results will be? These are questions to answer as they read.

To keep them involved in the story, suggest that students use a highlighter to mark phrases describing the results of Tim's taking steroids.

Side-Column Vocabulary Remind students that the vocabulary words and phrases in the side column have been selected as important to the theme and content of the story. These words may be useful in the context of steroid use and wellness, but they are not necessarily part of everyday language.

Mid-Passage Questions The answers to the questions mostly can be found in the text. Review students' written answers to assess whether they are getting meaning from the text. They should be able to point to evidence in the text to support all of their answers. Encourage them to underline or highlight that evidence. For example, they should note that Tim is discouraged because he is not getting the visible results he'd hoped for from his workouts. He also resents it when Ox tells him to stop using the steroids.

After You Read (PAGES 10–12)

Build a robust vocabulary. Ask students to check their answers in the answer keys in their books.

Think about your reading. Ask students to check their answers in the answer keys in their books. Ask additional questions to enrich the discussion so that students will be better able to write about solving personal health care issues. Here are some possible questions:

- A good reader "reads between the lines." What did the author want you to figure out from these sentences: *Tim kept staring at Ox. He watched the man strut. Tim wanted a body like that. Abruptly, he got up and walked over to him.* How is Tim feeling in this scene? What clues in the sentences tell you that he has made up his mind to do something? Have students identify the word *abruptly* as a hint that Tim made up his mind to act quickly.

- When Tim bought and used the steroids, he did not think about the consequences of putting chemicals and hormones into his body. In addition to Tim

becoming aggressive and losing his girlfriend, what else could have occurred because of Tim's using steroids? Help students consider what it would have been like if Tim had gotten into a fight and had been hurt. He also could have been in trouble with the law, since anabolic steroids are illegal.

Extend the reading. Here are some additional activities to expand students' understanding:

- This story provides some good opportunities for reading dialogues aloud. Tim and Meg's fight on page 9 or the exchange between Tim and Ox near the end of the story on page 9 may serve as scripts. Encourage students to read with as much natural expression as possible.

- *For English Language Learners* Have students reread page 7 and write the contractions they find. (*He'd, didn't, I'm, he's, don't, It'll, That's*) Discuss the two words that make up each contraction, and have students use these contractions in original sentences. Reframe the sentences that do not use the contractions correctly. Remind students to add these contractions to their personal dictionaries. Suggest that it is most appropriate to use contractions when they are writing and speaking informally.

- Point out to students that they make inferences all the time. Have students work in pairs to tell one another about something they did the previous weekend. After each speaker speaks, the listener shares one inference he or she made from the speaker's story. The speaker then tells the listener whether that inference was correct. You may wish to model this with a story of your own. For example: *We went to the mall because I don't like being outside when the weather is bad. I bought toys for my sons, and they were so excited.* Inferences: *The woman took her sons to the mall. Her sons liked the toys she bought for them.*

- At home, have students find and read articles in newspapers, in magazines, or on the Internet about anabolic steroid use. Alternatively, if students have access to someone who has used steroids, have students learn about that person's personal experience with steroids: Did they work? What were the side effects? Would they recommend steroid use to others? During the next class, have students share in small groups what they learned.

Use reading skills: Make inferences. Explain to students that everyone makes inferences as they are reading. Since writers do not and cannot state everything they mean to convey, it is often up to the reader to infer the author's meaning. They take what they know from the reading and what they know from their life experiences, and from that they make new meaning from the text. These are the inferences they draw.

Use a graphic organizer. In this lesson, the graphic organizer helps students observe how what they have read and what they know leads them to the inferences they make. This graphic organizer ensures that students are using both what they know and evidence from the text to support their inferences.

Write About It (PAGES 13–14)

Write a letter to the editor. Have students read the directions on page 13. Be sure they understand that they will write a letter to the editor expressing their opinions about steroid use.

Prewriting Remind students that real-life problems are often complex. Steroid use is an example of such a problem. Although many people are strongly opposed to steroid use, the people who use them have an advantage in many sports. Point out that the graphic organizer, a web, breaks the problem and its solutions into smaller parts. Tell students that thinking about smaller elements helps them to analyze the problem and to better organize their thinking about how to write about it. Encourage students to think and make notes about the problem and its possible solutions as comprehensively as possible. Filling in the circles in the web will provide essential details for a thoughtful letter to the editor.

Thinking Beyond Reading Have each student work with a partner or a small group to discuss the questions.

The intent is for students to probe more deeply and to elaborate on the topic by addressing issues that did not arise when they were first thinking about steroid use. Encourage them to add ideas to their webs.

Write a draft. Have students write independently. Write on the board the following sample topic sentence: *I believe that steroid use in recreational sports should be legal (or illegal.)* Be sure that students understand that all the sentences in the paragraph must relate to the same main idea, in this case whether or not steroid use should be allowed in recreational athletics. Remind students to use the ideas in their webs to organize the different elements of their responses. These will be the details in their paragraphs. While drafting, students should not be concerned with spelling or punctuation. Encourage them to write their thoughts quickly and freely.

Revise and create a final draft. Remind students to use the Revising and Editing Checklist (Master 11) to guide them in revising their writing. Have students review each other's writing and give each other feedback on the parts of their letters that are logical, clear, and interesting, and the parts that need revision.

When students have finished revising their writing, use the Writing Rubric (Master 10) to evaluate it. Be sure you review your response with each student so he or she understands the strengths and weaknesses of this piece of writing. Have students date the writing and put the completed pieces in their writing portfolios.

Building Fluency

Identify small sections from "Rage." Tell students that they will use paired reading to read these sections aloud. Put students into groups of two. Give them time to read a passage silently 2–3 times to encourage their best oral reading. Partners take turns being the reader or listener. After the first reading, the listener does not provide feedback. After the second and third readings, the listener provides feedback to the reader. Remind students to pay attention to words that cause them to stumble and to read for the author's message. Their goal is to read the passage as fluently as if they were just speaking.

On the Job

Lesson Overview: (PAGE 15)

Theme

Have students read the lesson title on page 15 and tell them that the title introduces the lesson theme, Work. Have students make personal connections, telling if they work, where they work, and what they do. Ask them if they have ever dealt with someone stealing at work.

Learning Objectives

Be sure students understand the outcome of each of the learning goals.

- *Read a story about a man's problem at work.* Point out that this story is fiction, but it deals with a real problem in the workplace.
- *Make judgments about the people in the story.*
- *Master the key vocabulary used in the story.*
- *Write an opinion paragraph about what a company should do about a worker who may be stealing.*

Preteach the vocabulary. (PAGE 15)

Read the key vocabulary words and their definitions to students. Tell them that they will recognize all these words in the story.

- Distribute the Vocabulary Knowledge Rating Chart (Master 9) and have students individually rate each of the key vocabulary words.
- Preview particularly challenging words with students by listing each one on the board, modeling its use in a sentence, and having two or three students use the word in original sentences. Reframe student sentences that do not use the new words correctly.

You may wish to offer a mini-lesson on verbs as students read the respective parts of speech with the definitions of the vocabulary words. [See page 40 of this book for a mini-lesson on verbs. Use Master 3 or 4 to give students practice in recognizing verbs.]

Before You Read (PAGE 16)

Explain to students that good readers learn to use different strategies as they read. Once they have mastered these strategies, they select the strategies that will work best with each of the texts they read. A good reader thinks about what he or she knows about the subject, for example, and visualizes what is going on in the story. Rereading will help reduce confusion about an element in the story's plot.

As students begin to write answers to the questions for each element on page 16, have them read the respective Think About Its.

Use what you know.   Use the Think About It to elicit discussion about students' individual work histories. Since each reader comes to a text with a different background, however, students' responses will be different. In this case, students will cite different problems at work and different ways to resolve those problems.

Preview the story.   Ask the students what the title of the story suggests to them. Ask them if the picture gives them more information. After reading the first three paragraphs, do students predict that Richard and Marco's relationship is going to change?

Reading the Story (PAGES 17–19)

Suggest that students read to find out what happens to two waiters as they do their jobs. It is a question to answer as they read. Visualizing what is going on in the story is a way to stay involved with the text.

Side-Column Vocabulary   Remind students that the vocabulary words and phrases in the side column have been selected as important to the theme and content of the story. These words may be useful in the context of the food-services industry, but they are not necessarily part of everyday language.

Mid-Passage Questions The answers to the questions are a combination of students' opinions and facts taken directly from the text. Regardless, students should be able to point to the places in their texts where they found their answers or evidence. Students should be able to articulate clearly from their own experience and opinions whether they feel Richard had a right to be angry at Marco and what Richard should do about the situation. Review students' written answers to assess whether they are getting meaning from the text.

After You Read (PAGES 20–22)

Build a robust vocabulary. Ask students to check their answers in the answer keys in their books.

Think about your reading. Ask students to check their answers in the answer keys in their books. Ask additional questions to enrich the discussion so that students will be better able to write about employee problems at work.

- A good reader "reads between the lines." What did the author want you to know about Richard from this sentence: "Richard drove his old battered Honda to work, parking in the lot behind the bistro." Why did it matter that Richard drove an older model car?

- Richard decided not to tell his boss or the other waiters about Marco's stealing. What is another decision he could have made? What might have been the consequences of that decision?

Extend the reading. Here are some additional activities to expand students' understanding.

- Encourage students to take parts and read the dialogues aloud. Richard's discussion with his wife on page 17 and Richard's confrontation on page 16 with Marco in the parking lot provide good opportunities for oral reading. Encourage students to read with as much natural expression as possible.

- *For English Language Learners* This story provides excellent examples of idiomatic language. Have students reread page 18 and look for the following phrases and expressions that don't mean exactly what the words say:

spelled trouble, What's up, pooled their tips, watched each other's back. Have students read the expressions in the context of the sentences and explain what they think the phrases mean. Model for them additional sentences that use the phrases correctly until students understand their proper usage in English. Have students try to use these phrases in original sentences. Reframe the sentences that do not use the phrase correctly. Remind students to add these phrases to their personal dictionaries.

- At home, have each student interview someone regarding dishonesty in the workplace. Have students create and ask questions (Examples: Have you ever been in a situation where someone was stealing where you work? Would you always turn someone in who was stealing? Would you ever consider taking something from your workplace?) Have students record the answers and report their findings to the class.

Use reading skills: Make judgments. Explain that experienced readers are able to read the author's text, combine it with what they know from their own experience, and make judgments about characters' actions and motivations. To a large extent, judgments depend on the reader's beliefs and values, although the author may also provide clues as to how he or she judges the characters' actions. Do students think that Marco was justified in being so angry? Do students think that in the end Richard will forgive Marco for his actions? Do students think that the author is sympathetic to Marco or to Richard? Which sentences show that?

Use a graphic organizer. In this lesson, the judgment chart visually organizes what the reader knows from the text and what the reader knows from his or her experience, then asks the reader to make a judgment about Marco's action. The chart helps the reader organize the information in smaller, manageable parts.

Write About It (PAGES 23–24)

Write an opinion paragraph. Have students read the directions on page 23. Be sure they understand that they will write their judgments about a waiter who is accused of stealing from the restaurant that employs him.

Prewriting Remind students that dealing with a situation with an employee is an example of a complex problem with more than one solution. Point out that the graphic organizer breaks down the information that the reader knows. Tell students that thinking about smaller elements will help them to analyze the problem and better organize their thoughts about what to do.

Thinking Beyond Reading Have each student work with a partner or a small group to discuss the questions. The intent is for students to probe more deeply and to elaborate on the topic by addressing issues that did not arise when they were first thinking about the situation with the waiter. Encourage them to add ideas to their charts.

Write a draft. Have students write independently. Be sure that students understand that all the sentences in the paragraph must relate to the same main idea, in this case their judgment about how to deal with Jack. Remind students to use the ideas in their charts to organize their responses. These will be the details in their paragraphs. While drafting, students should not be concerned with spelling or punctuation. Encourage them to write their thoughts quickly and freely.

Revise and create a final draft. Remind students to use the Revising and Editing Checklist (Master 11) to guide them in making revisions to their writing. Have students review each other's writing and give each other feedback on the parts of their paragraphs that are logical, clear, and interesting, and the parts that need revision.

When students have finished revising their writing, use the Writing Rubric (Master 10) to evaluate it. Be sure you review your response with each student so he or she understands the strengths and weaknesses of this piece of writing. Have students date the writing and put the completed pieces in their writing portfolios.

Building Fluency

Identify small sections from "Among Friends." Tell students that they will use paired reading to read these sections aloud. Put students into groups of two. Give them time to read a passage silently 2–3 times to encourage their best oral reading. Partners take turns being the reader or listener. After the first reading, the listener does not provide feedback. After the second and third readings, the listener provides feedback to the reader. Remind students to pay attention to words that cause them to stumble and to read for the author's message. Their goal is to read the passage as fluently as if they were just speaking.

We Are Family

Lesson Overview: (PAGE 25)

Theme

Have students read the lesson title on page 25 and tell them that the title introduces the lesson theme, Family. Have students make personal connections, telling if they have siblings and if so, how many. Ask them if they ever wished they had more or fewer siblings.

Learning objectives

Be sure students understand the outcome of each of the learning goals.

- *Learn about families with only one child.* Point out that the reading material is nonfiction and is based on facts.
- *Synthesize information.*
- *Master the key vocabulary used in the article.*
- *Write an explanation.*

Preteach the vocabulary. (PAGE 25)

Read the key vocabulary words and their definitions to the students. Tell them that they will recognize all these words in the article.

- Distribute the Vocabulary Knowledge Rating Chart (Master 9) and have students individually rate each of the key vocabulary words.
- Preview particularly challenging words with students by listing each one on the board, modeling its use in a sentence, and having two or three students use the word in original sentences. Reframe student sentences that do not use the new words correctly.

You may wish to offer a mini-lesson on nouns as students read the respective parts of speech with the definitions of the vocabulary words. [See page 39 of this book for a mini-lesson on nouns. Use Master 1 or 2 to give students practice in recognizing nouns.]

Before You Read (PAGE 26)

Explain that good readers know when they don't understand something and take steps to increase their understanding. Point out that good readers focus on the reading, putting question marks in the margin where they find things they do not understand. After marking a confusing passage, a good reader forms questions and then rereads to find the answers. Explain that context clues and a dictionary can help with confusing words. Rereading will also help with confusion about an idea in the article. Remind students that all of the strategies require writing and/or highlighting, so they should keep a pen or pencil, sticky notes or a notebook, and a highlighter on hand as they read.

As students begin to write answers to the questions for each element on page 26, have them read the respective Think About Its.

Use what you know. Have students read the Think About It. Ask if they have similar or different opinions about growing up with siblings. Would they have preferred to be only children in their families? By accessing their prior knowledge, this Think About It demonstrates how readers become more personally engaged with the text.

Ask yourself questions. Remind students that asking and answering questions as they read is a key strategy for increasing comprehension. Have students work in small groups to share and compare their answers with one another. Since one of the questions involves students' personal experiences, it should lead to interesting discussions that make personal connections.

Reading the Article (PAGES 27–29)

Emphasize to students that they will read to find out how only children's lives are different from the lives of children who have siblings. It is a question to answer as they read. Highlighting or marking phrases that show how the lives of only children are different is a strategy that will keep them involved in the article.

Side-Column Vocabulary Remind students that the vocabulary words and phrases in the side column have been selected as important to the theme and content of the story. These words may be useful in the context of families and children, but they are not necessarily part of everyday language.

Mid-Passage Questions The answers to the questions are largely from the text, so students should be able to point to evidence to support their answers. Encourage students to place a star next to the proof they find for their answers. Review students' written answers to assess whether they are getting meaning from the text.

After You Read (PAGES 30–32)

Build a robust vocabulary. Ask students to check their answers in the answer keys in their books.

Think about your reading. Ask students to check their answers in the answer keys in their books. Ask additional questions to enrich the discussion so that students will be better able to write about families and children. Here are some possible questions:

- A good author gets his or her audience involved in the text right from the beginning. Reread the first paragraph in this article. Why did the author choose to begin the passage with three questions? Did the strategy get you involved and interested in the text? Why or why not?

- The author says that only children tend to have more extensive verbal abilities than children with siblings, but she doesn't explain why this is so. Why do you think only children tend to have greater verbal abilities?

Extend the reading. Here are some additional activities to expand students' understanding:

- Have students compile a short list of questions to ask representatives from several different families, for example, *How many siblings do you have? Have you ever wished you had more or fewer siblings? Why?* At home, have students interview perhaps two adults and two children

each. Have students synthesize their findings and present them during the next class meeting.

- *For English Language Learners* Have students look through the last section of the article under the heading *More Results* and list examples of contractions (*what's, don't, that's, it's, wouldn't*). Have students write the two words that make up each contraction. Discuss with students times when it is and is not appropriate to use contractions. Then, have students use these and other contractions in original sentences.

- The reports in the article from the 42-year-old woman with one child (page 27), the seven-year-old (page 29), and the Texas man (page 29) provide good opportunities for oral reading. Encourage students to read with as much natural expression as they can. You may wish to encourage students to dramatize the parts by getting into the characters of the three different people. They may also wish to augment the quotations by adding life stories that students construct.

- Have students work in groups of 3–4 to discuss inflation and how money has affected or will affect their decisions about family size and other lifestyle issues. Then, have each member work individually to synthesize the discussion and the information the group provided. Have each student read aloud his or her synthesis, and have the group evaluate how well the synthesis reflected the discussion.

Use reading skills: Synthesize information. Explain to students that experienced readers are constantly synthesizing the information they are reading: They are looking for important information, retelling it in their own words, and forming new, slightly broader concepts based on the information. As readers continue, they add information to what they have already read or already know. This new information changes how they describe the concept or idea. In this article, for instance, students will first be informed by the reasons why family sizes are shrinking. But they are likely to have more personal responses when they read what research has shown about the differences in verbal abilities and happiness levels between onlies and children with brothers and sisters. These concepts will impact the way students synthesize the ideas in the article.

Use a graphic organizer. In this lesson, the synthesis chart visually displays how information from a passage can be combined with what a reader thinks and knows in order to become a broader concept. This graphic organizer allows the reader to see how synthesis takes place.

Write About It (PAGES 33–34)

Write an explanation. Have students read the directions on page 33. Be sure they understand that they will write to a neighbor telling how to encourage her daughter to socialize and to learn new skills.

Prewriting Remind students that they can find ideas for their writing both from their own experiences and from the article they have read about only children. Encourage students to reread the article and to highlight examples of how only children can socialize with each other. Students should use the graphic organizer to organize their thoughts for writing.

Thinking Beyond Reading Have each student work with a partner or a small group to discuss the questions. The intent is for students to probe more deeply and to elaborate on the topic by addressing issues that did not arise when they were first thinking about creating opportunities for the only child to socialize with other children. Encourage them to add ideas to their webs.

Write a draft. Have students write independently. Write on the board the following sample topic sentence: *There are*

different ways that only children can be encouraged to socialize with other children. Be sure that students understand that all the sentences in the paragraph must relate to the same main idea, in this case how only children can socialize with other children. Remind students to use the ideas in their charts to organize the different elements of their responses. The rows from the charts will be the details in their paragraphs. While drafting, students should not be concerned with spelling or punctuation. Encourage them to write their thoughts quickly and freely.

Revise and create a final draft. Remind students to use the Revising and Editing Checklist (Master 11) to guide them in revising their writing. Have students review each other's writing and give each other feedback on the parts of the paragraph that are logical, clear, and interesting, and the parts that need revision.

When students have finished revising their writing, use the Writing Rubric (Master 10) to evaluate it. Be sure you review your response with each student so he or she understands the strengths and weaknesses of this piece of writing. Have students date the writing and put the completed pieces in their writing portfolios.

Building Fluency

Identify small sections from "The Only Child." Tell students that they will use echo reading to read these sections aloud. Put students into groups of two. Give them time to read a passage silently 2–3 times to encourage their best oral reading. Remind them to pay attention to words that cause them to stumble. Remind students to use punctuation and typographic cues to add expression to their reading. Tell them that the goal is to read the passage as fluently as if they were just speaking.

Making a Comeback

Lesson Overview: (PAGE 35)

Theme

Have students read the lesson title on page 35 and tell them that the title introduces the lesson theme, Community. Have students make personal connections, telling what the town or community is like where they grew up. Ask them what people did for work there.

Learning Objectives

Be sure students understand the outcome of each of the learning goals.

- *Learn about a community that has gone through many changes.* Tell students that this article is nonfiction. It gives factual information about what happened in a real town that needed to change.
- *Identify main idea and details.*
- *Master the key vocabulary used in the article.*
- *Write a personal narrative about something that happened in your community.*

Preteach the vocabulary. (PAGE 35)

Read the key vocabulary words and their definitions to students. Tell them that they will recognize all these words in the article.

- Distribute the Vocabulary Knowledge Rating Chart (Master 9) and have students individually rate each of the key vocabulary words.
- Preview particularly challenging words with students by listing each one on the board, modeling its use in a sentence, and having two or three students use the word in original sentences. Reframe student sentences that do not use the new words correctly.

You may wish to offer a mini-lesson on adjectives as students read the respective parts of speech with the definitions of the vocabulary words. [See page 41 of this book for a mini-lesson on adjectives. Use Master 5 or 6 to give students practice in recognizing adjectives.]

Before You Read (PAGE 36)

Explain to students that by interacting with texts and getting involved with what they are reading, they will understand and remember more of what they read. Point out that good readers focus on the reading, putting question marks in the margin where they find ideas that they do not understand. After marking a confusing passage, a good reader forms questions and then rereads to find the answers.

As students begin to write answers to the questions for each element on page 36, have them read the respective Think About Its.

Use what you know. As students think about their own communities, have them read the Think About It and evaluate whether their answers to the questions are similar to the comments in the Think About It.

Set a purpose for reading. Remind students that nonfiction texts are written in order to share information. Why would information about the town of North Adams be important or interesting to share? Ask what information they think they can learn from this article and how they might be able to use it.

Reading the Article (PAGES 37–39)

Emphasize to students that they will read to find out how the town of North Adams, Massachusetts, made an economic comeback. It is a question to answer as they read. To keep them involved in the article, suggest that students highlight or mark sentences that describe the changes that took place in the town.

Side-Column Vocabulary Remind students that the vocabulary words and phrases in the side column have been selected as important to the theme and content of the article. These words may be useful in the context of community revitalization, but they are not necessarily part of everyday language.

Mid-Passage Questions The answers to the questions are largely stated in the text. Students should be able to identify the places in the text where they found their answers. Review students' answers to assess whether they are getting meaning from the text. Students may have differing opinions about whether the Sprague Electric Company was good for North Adams, but they should be able to support their opinions with evidence from the text.

After You Read (PAGES 40–42)

Build a robust vocabulary. Ask students to check their answers in the answer keys in their books.

Think about your reading. Ask students to check their answers in the answer keys in their books. Ask additional questions to enrich the discussion so that students will be better able to write about their communities. Here are some possible questions:

- Authors sometimes choose not to say everything directly and expect their readers to infer meaning from the text. At the end of the article, a man says, "The city doesn't have any money, but it's extremely rich." What do you think he means? Does the author leave the reader on an optimistic or a pessimistic note?

- There are ways to revitalize a community other than North Adam's solution of building a cultural center. What are some additional ways to revitalize a community?

Extend the reading. Here are some additional activities to expand students' understanding.

- Students may enjoy pretending that they are news reporters broadcasting a piece about North Adams's revival. Have partners write one or two paragraph summaries of the article. Then, have partners take turns reading the summaries as if they are on television. Encourage students to speak clearly and with expression, mimicking news reporters on the air.

- *For English Language Learners* Have students reread the second paragraph of the article.

Call attention to the five short sentences that end the paragraph. Model for students how to combine sentences using *and* and *so*. (*Businesses had closed, so people were unemployed; Businesses had closed and buildings were empty.*) Ask students to write four short, but related, sentences about their own communities and then exchange papers with a partner. Ask the partner to combine the sentences with *and* or *so* and read the new sentences aloud.

- At home, have students find articles in a newspaper about something that is happening in their communities. Have students summarize the articles and share the information during the next class. Have students discuss whether the articles show their communities in a positive or negative light.

Use reading skills: Identify main ideas and details. Experienced readers know that identifying the main idea and details is central to understanding a nonfiction article. It is an important part of the text structure, the way that the author organizes the story. Ask students to identify the author's main point in this article. How would students summarize the article to someone who hadn't read it? If the person who hadn't read the article asked for some specific details, which details would students choose to support that main idea?

Use a graphic organizer. The chart visually organizes the main idea and the supporting details for one paragraph in the article. The paragraph about the Sprague Electric Company serves as a bridge between the years before World War II and after the war. Sprague changed the history of the town during this period. This graphic organizer helps students analyze the text by looking at it in smaller, more manageable parts.

Write About It (PAGES 43–44)

Write a personal narrative. Have students read the directions on page 43. Be sure they understand they will each write a one-paragraph personal story about something that happened in their own life.

Prewriting   Remind students that they will focus on one event. Each will write a topic sentence that includes the key idea about the event, and then will support that statement with details about where the incident happened, who was there, and how the incident changed them. Using the graphic organizer will help students to identify details that directly support the main idea they want to communicate.

Thinking Beyond Reading   Have each student work with a partner or a small group to discuss the questions. The intent is for students to probe more deeply and to elaborate on their topics by addressing details that did not arise when they were first thinking about their events. Encourage them to add ideas to their graphic organizers.

Write a draft.   Have students write independently. Be sure that students understand that all the sentences in the paragraph must relate to the same main idea, in this case a particular incident. Remind students to use the ideas in their graphic organizer to organize their responses. These will be the details in their paragraphs. While drafting, students should not be concerned with spelling or punctuation. Encourage them to write their thoughts quickly and freely.

Revise and create a final draft.   Remind students to use the Revising and Editing Checklist (Master 11) to guide them in making revisions to their writing. Have students review each other's writing and give each other feedback on the parts of the paragraph that are logical, clear, and interesting, and the parts that need revision.

When students have finished revising their writing, use the Writing Rubric (Master 10) to evaluate it. Be sure you review your response with each student so he or she understands the strengths and weaknesses of this piece of writing. Have students date the writing and put the completed pieces in their writing portfolios.

Building Fluency

Identify small sections from "North Adams, Here We Come." Tell students that they will use paired reading to read these sections aloud. Put students into groups of two. Give them time to read a passage silently 2–3 times to encourage their best oral reading. Partners take turns being the reader or listener. After the first reading, the listener does not provide feedback. After the second and third readings, the listener provides feedback to the reader. Remind students to pay attention to words that cause them to stumble and to read for the author's message. Their goal is to read the passage as fluently as if they were just speaking.

Summer Vacations

Lesson Overview: (PAGE 45)

Theme

Have students read the lesson title on page 45 and tell them that the title introduces the lesson theme, School and Education. Have students make personal connections, telling what kinds of activities they did in school and what they did when they were not in school. Ask them if they or anyone they know went to summer camp when they were children.

Learning objectives

Be sure students understand the outcome of each of the learning goals.

- *Learn about summer camps for children.* Point out that this article presents various and unique summer camps. It is nonfiction, and it describes each real camp experience.
- *Distinguish between fact and opinion.*
- *Master the key vocabulary used in the article.*
- *Write a description.*

Preteach the vocabulary. (PAGE 45)

Have students take turns reading the key vocabulary words and their definitions on page 45. Tell them that they will recognize all these words in the article.

- Distribute the Vocabulary Knowledge Rating Chart (Master 9) and have students individually rate each of the key vocabulary words.
- Preview particularly challenging words with students by listing each one on the board, modeling its use in a sentence, and having two or three students use the word in original sentences. Reframe student sentences that do not use the new words correctly.

You may wish to offer a mini-lesson on verbs as students read the respective parts of speech with the definitions of the vocabulary words. [See page 40 of this book for a

mini-lesson on verbs. Use Master 3 or 4 to give students practice in recognizing verbs.]

Before You Read (PAGE 46)

Explain that good readers constantly ask themselves questions as they read. They ask questions about the text to clarify the meaning. Usually, they ask and answer many of those questions in their heads. As students work to focus on reading skills, however, it is a good idea to record questions in the margins or on sticky notes. After marking a confusing passage, a good reader will reread to find the answers to his or her questions.

As students begin to write answers to the questions for each element on page 46, have them read the respective Think About Its.

Use what you know. Use the Think About It to elicit discussion with students about how they spend their time off and the vacation trips they have taken. Ask them to compare their responses to the Think About It. Do they share the idea of needing a change of pace?

Ask yourself questions. Have students write their questions on sticky notes so that they will be able to go back to them after they've finished reading the three paragraphs. Do they relate to the idea of learning skills at camp? Do they wonder what kinds of skills kids learn? Remind students that asking questions is a strategy to keep them involved in the reading. Encourage students to have pens, sticky notes, and highlighters handy as they read.

Reading the Article (PAGES 47–49)

Emphasize to students that they will read to find out what kinds of summer camps there are and who goes to them. It is a question to answer as they read. To keep them involved in the article, suggest that students use a highlighter to mark sentences that describe different kinds of camps for children with different kinds of needs.

Side-Column Vocabulary Remind students that the vocabulary words and phrases in the side column have been selected as important to the theme and content of the article. These words may be useful in the context of summer camp and campers' different physical and emotional needs, but they are not necessarily part of everyday language.

Mid-Passage Questions The answers to the questions are largely stated in the text. Students should be able to identify the sentences that answer the questions. Students should also be able to back up their opinions when responding to questions with answers that are not explicitly stated. Do they recognize that some children cry when they are frightened about new experiences? Review students' written answers to assess whether they are getting meaning from the text.

After You Read (PAGES 50–52)

Build a robust vocabulary. Ask students to check their answers in the answer keys in their books.

Think about your reading. Ask students to check their answers in the answer keys in their books. Ask additional questions to enrich the discussion so that students will be better able to write about children attending different kinds of camps. Here are some possible questions:

- Sometimes, authors do not include all of the details that a reader might want. In these cases, it is up to the reader to infer, or figure out, what the author did not say. In the *Hole in the Wall* section of the article, the author says that some children are too ill to go to camp. For those children, *Counselors from Camp-in-a-Suitcase create the flavor of camp.* Ask students this question: *From what you know about camp, what do you think Camp-in-a-Suitcase could be?*

- In the article, there appear to be different categories of camps. How could the types of camps in the article be categorized? What are some differences between camps for children who are well and camps for children who have special needs?

  Extend the reading. Here are some additional activities to expand students' understanding:

- Have students work in small groups and take turns describing a child. The listeners should use the information about the child to suggest one of the camps described in the article. If members of the group disagree, have them use facts in the article to support their positions.

- *For English Language Learners* Extend the suffix lesson by having students find examples of words with the suffixes -al, -ful, -ly, and -ness in other articles. Students should determine the meanings of the words and then use them in sentences. If students are misusing or misunderstanding words, redirect them.

- Have pairs of students reread the article and look for statements that are facts and statements that are opinions. Tell them to mark the sentences with either an F (Fact) or an O (Opinion). Have the pairs share their lists with the class. Be sure students understand that a fact needs to have strong proof to back it up.

- At home, have students find advertisements, brochures, and web sites for children's summer camps. Have students record which children the camp is intended for, how long a session is, and what kinds of activities are available. During the next class, have students share what they learned and whether they discovered anything new about camps.

Use reading skills: Distinguish fact and opinion. Explain to students that experienced readers understand that it is important to be able to distinguish facts from opinions in an article. Remind them that opinions are beliefs that cannot be proven; facts can be proven with irrefutable evidence. Warn students that authors and speakers will often try to make their opinions seem like facts in an effort to persuade the reader or listener. It is the reader's responsibility to look for the evidence that supports a claim in order to determine if the statement is, indeed, a fact. It is equally important that writers provide strong evidence to support the facts they present.

Use a graphic organizer. In this lesson, the fact/opinion chart helps the reader to separate visually the facts from opinions in the article. Does the article show a balance between facts and opinions? Are there some sentences that are hard to classify? How, for instance, do students classify this sentence: *For sure, you'll come away with new abilities and knowledge you can use both in and out of school.* Why does the author say *For sure?* Does that phrase introduce a fact or an opinion?

Write About It (PAGES 53–54)

Write a description.   Have students read the directions on page 53. Be sure they understand that they will write a letter stating their opinion about sending Max to camp for two weeks.

Prewriting   Point out that the sister is asking for the students' help because she wants an "expert" opinion of what's best for her son. Remind students that facts are more convincing than opinions, so it is important that they use evidence from the text to support their opinions. Encourage students to think and make notes in the fact and opinion chart about the situation as comprehensively as possible. Providing a balance of facts and opinions will make their letters stronger and more convincing.

Thinking Beyond Reading   Have each student work with a partner or a small group to discuss the questions. The intent is for students to probe more deeply and to elaborate on the topic by addressing issues that did not arise when they were first thinking about whether or not the sister should send Max to camp. Encourage them to add facts and opinions to their charts.

Write a draft.   Have students write independently. Write on the board the following opening sentence: *I know that you are thinking of sending Max to camp.* Be sure that students understand that all the sentences in the paragraph must relate to the same main idea, in this case

whether or not to send Max to camp. Remind students to use the ideas in their fact and opinion charts to organize the different elements of their responses. These will be the details in their paragraphs. While drafting, students should not be concerned with spelling or punctuation. Encourage them to write their thoughts quickly and freely.

Revise and create a final draft.   Remind students to use the Revising and Editing Checklist (Master 11) to guide them in revising their writing. Have students review each other's writing and give each other feedback on the parts of the letter that are logical, clear, and interesting, and the parts that need revision.

When students have finished revising their writing, use the Writing Rubric (Master 10) to evaluate it. Be sure you review your response with each student so he or she understands the strengths and weaknesses of this piece of writing. Have students date the writing and put the completed pieces in their writing portfolios.

Building Fluency

Identify small sections from "What Happens at Summer Camp?" Tell students that they will use choral reading to read these sections aloud. (See page 7 of this book for a description of choral reading.) Give them time to read a passage silently 2–3 times to encourage the best oral reading. In order to set and maintain the pace, read along with the students. Identify words that cause the students to stumble. They will imitate the phrasing and intonation that you model. Remind students to use punctuation and typographic cues to add expression to their reading. Tell them that the goal is to read the passage as fluently as if they were just speaking.

Help in an Emergency

Lesson Overview: (PAGE 55)

Theme

Have students read the lesson title on page 55 and tell them that the title introduces the lesson theme, Civics and Government. Have students make personal connections, telling who the first responders are in their communities. Ask them if they know any first responders personally or if they have ever been in an emergency situation that required emergency personnel.

Learning Objectives

Be sure students understand the outcome of each of the learning goals.

- *Read a story about firefighters and others who arrive first at a disaster scene.* Point out that this is a fictional account of a fire. The author has made up the characters and the events, but they are true to what a serious fire is like and what firefighters actually do.

- *Identify cause and effect.*

- *Master the key vocabulary used in the story.*

- *Write a summary of the story.*

Preteach the vocabulary. (PAGE 55)

Read the key vocabulary words and their definitions to students. Tell them that they will recognize all these words in the story.

- Distribute the Vocabulary Knowledge Rating Chart (Master 9) and have students individually rate each of the key vocabulary words.

- Preview particularly challenging words with students by listing each one on the board, modeling its use in a sentence, and having two or three students use the word in original sentences. Reframe student sentences that do not use the new words correctly.

You may wish to offer a mini-lesson on adverbs as students read the respective parts of speech with the definitions of the vocabulary words. [See page 42 of this book for a mini-lesson on adverbs. Use Master 7 or 8 to give students practice in recognizing adverbs.]

Before You Read (PAGE 56)

Explain that good readers know when they don't understand something, and they take steps to increase understanding. They focus on the reading, putting question marks in the margin where they find ideas they do not understand. After marking a confusing passage, a good reader forms questions and then rereads to find the answers. Explain that context clues and a dictionary can help with confusing words. Rereading will also help with confusion about an element in the story's plot.

As students begin to write answers to the questions for each element on page 56, have them read the respective Think About Its.

Make predictions. What predictions have students made? Point out that they should check to see if their predictions are correct as they read the story.

Visualize while you read. Explain that good readers visualize the characters and the action in a story to help them follow what is happening. Have students read the second paragraph and discuss with a partner the pictures they have in their minds. Then, have students read the Think About It and compare their own visualizations with the Think About It visualization.

Reading the Story (PAGES 57–59)

Emphasize to students that they will read to find out if James Pasquini's extreme courage will be successful or wasted as he tries to save lives. It is a question to answer as they read. To keep them involved in the story, suggest that students put an asterisk in the margin when they find sentences that tell the outcomes of James's attempts to save two people.

Side-Column Vocabulary Remind students that the vocabulary words and phrases in the side column have been selected as important to the theme and content of the story. These words may be useful in the context of emergency personnel and fires, but they are not necessarily part of everyday language.

Mid-Passage Questions Some of the answers to the questions call on students' judgments, so there are not many right or wrong answers. Other responses to the questions can be found in the text, so students should be able to identify the sentences in which they found their answers. Review students' written answers to assess whether they are getting meaning from the text. They should indicate in their answers that this is a particularly dangerous chemical fire and the firefighting team doesn't have much information about the plant or the machinery in the plant.

After You Read (PAGES 60–62)

Build a robust vocabulary. Ask students to check their answers in the answer keys in their books.

Think about your reading. Ask students to check their answers in the answer keys in their books. Ask additional questions to enrich the discussion so that students will be better able to write from James Pasquini's point of view about what happened in the fire. Here are some possible questions:

- The author contrasts the workers with the first responders when she writes things like: ". . . workers ran in circles in blind panic" and "It didn't take long for Pasquini to make up his mind." Which qualities does Pasquini demonstrate during this story that make him a good first responder? Are these qualities found in most people, or are some people particularly well-suited for this role?

- James Pasquini had choices other than to run into the fire and rescue the two workers. What else could he have done? Why do you think: "Pasquini

hid a smile of triumph" when the other firefighters congratulated him?

Extend the reading. Here are some additional activities to expand students' understanding.

- Encourage students to take parts and read the dialogues aloud. The captain's talk to the firefighters on page 58 provides a good opportunity for oral reading. Remind students to read with as much natural expression as possible.

- *For English Language Learners* Remind students that compound words are two smaller words that form one longer word. Usually the word they form is related in meaning to the component words. Have students find compound words in the story (e.g. *firehouse, firefighters, headache, somewhere, whatever.*) Examine those words to see how the component words are related to the meaning of the compound word. Have students practice recognizing compound words by finding them in another article as well.

- Have pairs of students create another Cause and Effect chart and fill in either the cause or the effect of an event in "Burning." Then have each pair switch with another pair and complete each other's charts. Have the groups reconvene to discuss their responses.

- At home, have each student find an article in a newspaper or magazine about an emergency situation that occurred either locally or elsewhere. Tell them to read the article and write a summary of the article. Have them share their summaries orally in the next class.

Use reading skills: Identify cause and effect. Explain to students that when readers seek out the "whys" (the causes) and the results (the effects) of particular actions in a story, they get a clearer sense of the motivations of the characters and the chains of events that have occurred.

Use a graphic organizer. This chart visually organizes the causes and effects of three particular moments in the story. Understanding what caused the loud boom and the concerns about the toxicity of the fumes is at the heart of the story—why this fire is so frightening. Similarly, what results from the moans that Pasquini hears is important to his next decisions. The effects shape our views of Pasquini as a character.

Write About It (PAGES 63–64)

Write a summary. Have students read the directions on page 63. Be sure they understand that they will write a summary that includes only the most important events from the story. Extra details should be left out of a summary.

Prewriting Encourage students to use the Beginning, Middle, End chart to simplify and order the events in the story. If students write each of the important events on a sticky note, they will be able to add, delete, and re-order those events.

Thinking Beyond Reading Have each student work with a partner or a small group to discuss the questions. The intent is for students to either elaborate on or tweak their Beginning, Middle, and End sentences. Encourage students to add to or delete from their charts as necessary.

Write a draft. Have students write independently. Remind students to use the ideas in their charts to organize their responses. These important ideas will function as details in their summaries. They should be organized in the order they happened. While drafting, students should not be concerned with spelling or punctuation. Encourage them to write their thoughts quickly and freely.

Revise and create a final draft. Remind students to use the Revising and Editing Checklist (Master 11) to guide them in making revisions to their writing. Have students review each other's writing and give each other feedback on the parts of their summaries that are logical, clear, and interesting, and the parts that need revision.

When students have finished revising their writing, use the Writing Rubric (Master 10) to evaluate it. Be sure you review your response with each student so he or she understands the strengths and weaknesses of this piece of writing. Have students date the writing and put the completed pieces in their writing portfolios.

Building Fluency

Identify small sections from "Burning." Tell students that they will use paired reading to read these sections aloud. Put students into groups of two. Give them time to read a passage silently 2–3 times to encourage their best oral reading. Partners take turns being the reader or listener. After the first reading, the listener does not provide feedback. After the second and third readings, the listener provides feedback to the reader. Remind students to pay attention to words that cause them to stumble and to read for the author's message. Their goal is to read the passage as fluently as if they were just speaking.

A Sports Icon

Lesson Overview: (PAGE 65)

Theme

Have students read the lesson title on page 65 and tell them that the title introduces the lesson theme, Sports and Recreation. Have students make personal connections, identifying their favorite sports to watch and to play. Ask them if they have favorite sports heroes.

Learning Objectives

Be sure students understand the outcome of each of the learning goals.

- *Learn about golfer Tiger Woods.* Point out that this article is nonfiction. It tells the story of a real person. The events are true.
- *Recognize time order.*
- *Master the key vocabulary used in the article.*
- *Write about the people and events that influenced a person's life.*

Preteach the vocabulary. (PAGE 65)

Read the key vocabulary words and their definitions to the students. Tell them that they will recognize all these words in the article.

- Distribute the Vocabulary Knowledge Rating Chart (Master 9) and have students individually rate each of the key vocabulary words.
- Preview particularly challenging words with students by listing each one on the board, modeling its use in a sentence, and having two or three students use the word in original sentences. Reframe student sentences that do not use the new words correctly.

You may wish to offer a mini-lesson on verbs as students read the respective parts of speech with the definitions of the vocabulary words. [See page 40 of this book for a mini-lesson on verbs. Use Master 3 or 4 to give students practice in recognizing verbs.]

Before You Read (PAGE 66)

Explain that good readers know when they do not fully understand ideas in a passage, and they take steps to increase their understanding. When a passage is confusing, a reader often puts question marks in the margin, and rereads to find the answers to his or her questions. Remind students that when they summarize as they read, they recall the important events and main ideas in a passage. Summarizing as they are reading will make them aware of any gaps they have in their understanding or information they have missed.

As students begin to write answers to the questions for each element on page 66, have them read the Think About It.

Use what you know. Use the Think About It about Michael Jordan to elicit discussion about students' favorite sports and sports heroes. Different students may have very different favorite teams and players. Encourage them to explain *why* those teams and players are their favorites. As they read the title and look at the illustration on page 67, have them consider what they already know about Tiger Woods. Find out if students already know about his persistence when learning golf as a very young child. Do they know the other values that his parents taught him and how he lives those values today?

Summarize. Have students read the first two paragraphs of the article with the intention of pulling out the main point, that Tiger Woods is a sports hero to people around the world. Then, have students read the third paragraph and work in pairs to summarize the main idea in one sentence. Have pairs share and compare their sentences with others in the class.

Reading the Article (PAGES 67–69)

Emphasize to students that they will read to find out the important things that have happened in Tiger Woods' life and career. It is a question to answer as they read.

Jotting down the important events is a strategy that will keep them involved in the article as they read.

Side-Column Vocabulary Remind students that the vocabulary words and phrases in the side column have been selected as important to the theme and content of the article. These words may be useful in the context of sports and sports heroes, but they are not necessarily part of everyday language.

Mid-Passage Questions The answers to the questions are stated explicitly in the text. Review students' written answers to assess whether they are getting meaning from the text. Students should be able to point to the sentences where they found their answers. Students should recognize that Tiger was called a *prodigy* by the media a few years after he appeared on TV at the age of two.

After You Read (PAGES 70–72)

Build a robust vocabulary. Ask students to check their answers in the answer keys in their books.

Think about your reading. Ask students to check their answers in the answer keys in their books. Ask additional questions to enrich the discussion so that students will be better able to write about sports, sports teams, and sports heroes. Here are some possible questions:

- A good reader "reads between the lines." What does Tiger Woods' father mean when he says: *The only thing better than a good person is an educated person?* In what ways is Tiger Woods different from some other athletes you know about?

- This author chose to write about a particular athlete, Tiger Woods, rather than writing about sports heroes in general. Which athlete would you write about if you were the author? Why?

Extend the reading. Here are some additional activities to expand students' understanding:

- Have students pretend they are news reporters interviewing Tiger Woods. Have partners work together to write interview questions for

which the answers can be found in the article. Have one partner be the interviewer and the other partner be Tiger Woods answering the questions. Encourage students to speak clearly as they conduct their interviews for the class.

- *For English Language Learners* Have students find adjectives in "Who is Tiger Woods?" and then create their own sentences using the comparative and the superlative forms of each of those words. Assist students in adding inflectional endings, changing spellings, or adding *more* or *most*. Following is a list of adjectives from the text that you can present to students if they have difficulty finding words: *remarkable, courageous, strong, valuable, great, important.*

- Guide students in a discussion about the life events of someone who is familiar to all of them. Draw on the board a time line like the one on page 72 and have students help you to write the important events onto the time line.

- At home, have each student find a printed advertisement or a TV commercial that shows a celebrity endorsing a particular product. Have students write short paragraphs telling who the celebrity is, what product he or she is endorsing, and why they think the celebrity is endorsing that particular product. Have students share their paragraphs in small groups during the next class.

Use reading skills: Recognize time order. Explain to students that experienced readers recognize that not every text is organized in chronological order. Even when the events are in chronological order, important events are not necessarily spaced out evenly in the text. It may be important to keep track of events to be able to recognize how they affect and shape a person's successes, failures, and the development of character. In the case of "Who is Tiger Woods?," the events are chronological.

Use a graphic organizer. In this lesson, the time line visually illustrates the events in Tiger Woods' life and helps the reader to see how earlier events affected later events. In the case of Tiger Woods, a time line also helps the reader to see just how much this athlete has accomplished in a very short time.

Write About It (PAGES 73–74)

Write about the people and events that influenced a person's life. Have students read the directions on page 73. Be sure they understand that they will each write a paragraph describing a person they respect for his or her admirable character traits.

Prewriting Remind students that character development is not a simple process. There are many people and events that influence a person's character. Tell students that thinking about discrete influences will help them identify the person's character traits and examine how each developed. This will help them write in an organized manner so that their sentences logically follow each other. Have students use the time line to help them organize their paragraphs.

Thinking Beyond Reading Have each student work with a partner or a small group to discuss the questions. The intent is for students to probe more deeply and to elaborate on the topic by identifying events and people who did not come to mind when they were first thinking about the person. Encourage them to add ideas to their time lines.

Write a draft. Have students write independently. Be sure that they understand that all the sentences in their paragraphs must relate to their main ideas. Remind students to use the ideas in their time lines to organize the

different elements of their responses. These will be the details in their paragraphs. While drafting, students should not be concerned with spelling or punctuation. Encourage them to write their thoughts quickly and freely.

Revise and create a final draft. Remind students to use the Revising and Editing Checklist (Master 11) to guide them in revising their writing. Have students review each other's writing and give each other feedback on the parts of their paragraphs that are logical, clear, and interesting, and the parts that need revision.

When students have finished revising their writing, use the Writing Rubric (Master 10) to evaluate it. Be sure you review your response with each student so he or she understands the strengths and weaknesses of this piece of writing. Have students date the writing and put the completed pieces in their writing portfolios.

Building Fluency

Identify small sections from "Who Is Tiger Woods?" Tell students that they will use paired reading to read these sections aloud. Put students into groups of two. Give them time to read a passage silently 2–3 times to encourage their best oral reading. Partners take turns being the reader or listener. After the first reading, the listener does not provide feedback. After the second and third readings, the listener provides feedback to the reader. Remind students to pay attention to words that cause them to stumble and to read for the author's message. Their goal is to read the passage as fluently as if they were just speaking.

Flying High

Lesson Overview: (PAGE 75)

Theme

Have students read the lesson title on page 75 and tell them that the title introduces the lesson theme, Housing and Transportation. Have students make personal connections, telling about their experiences with airplanes and flying. Ask them whether or not they have heard of Amelia Earhart and what they know about her.

Learning Objectives

Be sure students understand the outcome of each of the learning goals.

- *Learn about Amelia Earhart's contributions to aviation.* Tell students this article is nonfiction, giving facts about the life of this famous woman.
- *Draw conclusions from the article.*
- *Master the key vocabulary used in the article.*
- *Write a letter to the editor.*

Preteach the vocabulary. (PAGE 75)

Read the key vocabulary words and their definitions to students. Tell them that they will recognize all these words in the article.

- Distribute the Vocabulary Knowledge Rating Chart (Master 9) and have students individually rate each of the key vocabulary words.
- Preview particularly challenging words with students by listing each one on the board, modeling its use in a sentence, and having two or three students use the word in original sentences. Reframe student sentences that do not use the new words correctly.

You may wish to offer a mini-lesson on nouns as students read the respective parts of speech with the definitions of the vocabulary words. [See page 39 of this book for a mini-lesson on nouns. Use Master 1 or 2 to give students practice in recognizing nouns.]

Before You Read (PAGE 76)

Point out that a good reader forms questions and then rereads to find the answers. Rereading will also help with confusion about a concept in the text. Explain also that using context clues and a dictionary can help with confusing words.

As students begin to write answers to the questions for each element on page 76, have them read the respective Think About Its.

Use what you know. Use the Think About It to elicit discussion about students' knowledge of Amelia Earhart. Since different people have different experiences, the Think About It will not mirror exactly what the student is thinking, but it provides a useful example. Continue with the other questions: Do students recall the first time they flew? Would they like to pilot a plane?

Ask yourself questions. Have students read the questions and then read the first two paragraphs of the article, keeping those questions in mind. Have students answer the questions individually, pointing to the sentences in the text where they found their answers. Then have partners discuss and compare their answers.

Reading the Article (PAGES 77–79)

Suggest that students read to learn about Amelia Earhart's contribution to the field of aviation. What her accomplishments were is a question to answer as they read. To keep them involved in the article, suggest that students highlight or mark sentences in the text that answer this question.

Side-Column Vocabulary Remind students that the vocabulary words and phrases in the side column have been selected as important to the theme and content of the article. These words may be useful in the context of aviation and transportation, but they are not necessarily part of everyday language.

Mid-Passage Questions The answers to most of the questions can be found in the text. Students should be able to point to the place in the text where they have found each of their answers. Review students' written answers to assess whether they are getting meaning from the text. They should be able to tell which words they would use to describe Earhart's life and career with evidence from the text.

After You Read (PAGES 80–82)

Build a robust vocabulary. Ask students to check their answers in the answer keys in their books.

Think about your reading. Ask students to check their answers in the answer keys in their books. Ask additional questions to enrich the discussion so that students will be better able to write about the importance of Amelia Earhart. Here are some possible questions:

- Sometimes authors slip details into their texts. This strategy informs the reader without calling a lot of attention to that information. How did the author tell the reader that Amelia Earhart was married and who her husband was? How did the author tell the reader that Amelia Earhart had nearly made it around the world before her plane disappeared on her last adventure? Have students find the answers in the text.

- The mystery surrounding Amelia Earhart's death is of great interest to many people. Why do you think the author of this passage chose to focus more on Earhart's life and accomplishments rather than on the circumstances surrounding her death?

Extend the reading. Here are some additional activities to expand students' understanding.

- Suggest that students take turns reading aloud and summarizing the paragraphs or sections in "The Disappearance of Amelia Earhart." Have listeners summarize the text that the reader has covered.

- *For English Language Learners* Have students reread the section entitled *Gaining Recognition.*

Tell them to look for the following phrases and expressions that don't mean exactly what the words say: *broke a record, made history,* and *ate lightly.* Have students read the expressions in the context of the sentences and explain what they think the phrases mean. Model for them additional sentences that use the phrases correctly until students understand their proper usage in English. Have students try to use these phrases in original sentences. Reframe the sentences that do not use the phrase correctly. Remind students to add these phrases to their personal dictionaries.

- Guide students in a discussion about conclusions that can be drawn from facts in the article. Draw on the board a chart like the one on page 84 and have small groups of students support a conclusion with facts they identify in the passage. Have the groups discuss and compare their charts.

- At home, have each student find an article in a newspaper or magazine about someone who has accomplished something "against the odds." Tell students to read the article, bring it to class, and prepare to summarize it orally for the class. Remind students to focus on the challenge that person overcame.

Use reading skills: Draw conclusions. Experienced readers take the facts the author provides and draw conclusions about a situation or a character's actions and motivations. Sometimes an author will provide a conclusion, and the reader must determine if there are enough relevant and compelling facts to agree with that conclusion. Encourage students to be aware of the conclusions they draw as they read "The Disappearance of Amelia Earhart" as well as the conclusions the author draws.

Use a graphic organizer. The chart visually organizes related facts in the text to show how those facts lead to conclusions. In this case, the writer has drawn a conclusion about Amelia Earhart's focus and determination, and students are asked to find in the article the facts that support that conclusion.

Write About It (PAGES 83–84)

Write a letter to the editor. Have students read the directions on page 83. Be sure students understand that they will pretend that they are living in 1937 and writing an opinion letter about Amelia Earhart's attempted plane trip around the world.

Prewriting Remind students that a letter to the editor expresses the writer's opinion and is supported by facts. The letter should be brief and to the point, presenting the facts and the conclusions one has drawn from the newspaper article. Tell students that their goal is to convince the reader that their point of view is correct, so they want to make a few persuasive points. Point out that the graphic organizer, a fact/conclusions chart, provides a way to organize facts and come to a conclusion. This will help students to write their letters so that their sentences all relate to the conclusion.

Thinking Beyond Reading Have students work with partners or small groups to discuss their facts and conclusions. The intent is for students to probe more deeply and to elaborate on the topic by addressing issues that did not arise when they were first thinking about Amelia Earhart's journey. Encourage them to add or delete ideas in their charts.

Write a draft. Have students write independently. Be sure that students understand that all the sentences in the paragraph must relate to the same main idea, in this case their opinion of Earhart's decision to fly around the world. Remind students to use the ideas in their charts to organize their responses. While drafting, students should not be concerned with spelling or punctuation. Encourage them to write their thoughts quickly and freely.

Revise and create a final draft. Remind students to use the Revising and Editing Checklist (Master 11) to guide them in making revisions to their writing. Have students review each other's writing and give each other feedback on the parts of their letters that are logical, clear, and interesting, and the parts that need revision.

When students have finished revising their writing, use the Writing Rubric (Master 10) to evaluate it. Be sure you review your response with each student so he or she understands the strengths and weaknesses of this piece of writing. Have students date the writing and put the completed pieces in their writing portfolios.

Building Fluency

Identify small sections from "The Disappearance of Amelia Earhart." Tell students that they will use paired reading to read these sections aloud. Put students into groups of two. Give them time to read a passage silently 2–3 times to encourage their best oral reading. Partners take turns being the reader or listener. After the first reading, the listener does not provide feedback. After the second and third readings, the listener provides feedback to the reader. Remind students to pay attention to words that cause them to stumble and to read for the author's message. Their goal is to read the passage as fluently as if they were just speaking.

Where Did That Fish Come From?

Lesson Overview: (PAGE 85)

Theme

Have students read the lesson title on page 85 and tell them that the title introduces the lesson theme, Food. Discuss the theme by having students make personal connections, telling if they enjoy eating fish; if so, where do they get it from? Have students share if they have ever been to a large distribution center for a product like fish, meat, or flowers.

Learning Objectives

Be sure students understand the outcome of each of the learning goals.

- *Learn about a famous fish market.* Provide background about the article by explaining that it is nonfiction and contains information about real people and real events.
- *Compare and contrast.*
- *Master the key vocabulary used in the article.*
- *Write a comparison.*

Preteach the vocabulary. (PAGE 85)

Read the key vocabulary words and their definitions to students. Tell them that they will recognize all these words in the article.

- Distribute the Vocabulary Knowledge Rating Chart (Master 9) and have students individually rate each of the key vocabulary words.
- Preview particularly challenging words with students by listing each one on the board, modeling its use in a sentence, and having two or three students use the word in original sentences. Reframe student sentences that do not use the new words correctly.

You may wish to offer a mini-lesson on adjectives as students read the respective parts of speech with the definitions of the vocabulary words. [See page 41 of this book for a mini-lesson on adjectives. Use Master 5 or 6 to give students practice in recognizing adjectives.]

Before You Read (PAGE 86)

Explain that good readers know when they don't understand something, and they take steps to increase their understanding. When a topic is new and mostly unfamiliar, a reader has to work harder to make meaning from the text. Having prior knowledge helps readers to remember more of what they read. Good readers focus on the reading, putting question marks in the margin when they find ideas they do not understand. After marking a confusing passage, a good reader forms questions and then rereads to find the answers. Explain that context clues and a dictionary can help with confusing words.

As students begin to write answers to the questions for each element on page 86, have them read the respective Think About Its.

Use what you know. Use the Think About It about eating fish to elicit discussion about the fish dishes that students like best, people who do not like to eat fish, and how students think fish gets to restaurants.

Visualize while you are reading. Have students read the first two paragraphs under the heading *State of the Art* and then describe what the new fish market looks like. Encourage students to include as much detail as possible in their visualizations. Explain that visualizing the places in the article will help them follow and remember what is happening.

Reading the Article (PAGES 87–89)

Emphasize to students that they will be reading to find out what they can learn about a new fish market. It is a question to answer as they read. To keep them involved in the article, suggest that students use a highlighter to mark sentences that contain information new to them.

Side-Column Vocabulary Remind students that the vocabulary words and phrases in the side column have been selected as important to the theme and content of the article. These words may be useful in the context of markets, but they are not necessarily part of everyday language.

Mid-Passage Questions The answers to most of the questions are explicitly stated in the text, so students should be able to identify the sentences in the article where they found their answers. Review students' written answers to assess whether they are getting meaning from the text.

After You Read (PAGES 90–92)

Build a robust vocabulary. Ask students to check their answers in the answer keys in their books.

Think about your reading. Ask students to check their answers in the answer keys in their books. Ask additional questions to enrich the discussion so that students will be better able to write about old and new markets. Here are some possible questions:

- A good reader sometimes uses additional resources to supplement the information provided in a text. Use a map to find where New York City is located and where the new Fulton Fish Market is in the Bronx. Using what you see on the map, what you know about that particular area, and what you have learned from the text, list and explain the factors that contribute to the Fulton Fish Market being so successful.

- Fulton Fish Market provides fish to restaurants and distributors in New York, New Jersey, and Connecticut. Find the name of a large distributor that provides food products, flowers, or cloth to retailers near where you live.

Extend the reading. Here are some additional activities to expand students' understanding:

- Have students pretend they are news reporters doing a story on the Fulton Fish Market. Have pairs of students reread the text, highlighting

the information about the Fulton Fish Market that tells *who, what, where, why, when,* and *how.* Then, have students write a paragraph describing the market, including its purpose, location, users, and what makes it unique. Finally, have students read their "reports" as if they are delivering news broadcasts.

- *For English Language Learners* Have partners take turns reading and summarizing paragraphs from the text. As one person reads, the other summarizes orally; then, each writes a summary sentence. After each partner has read and summarized one of the sections from the text, have them read their sentences aloud to the class.

- Have students work in pairs to discuss a situation in their everyday lives in which they are required to draw conclusions. Examples might be driving a car, ordering food at a restaurant, negotiating with a child or partner, or applying for a job. Have partners choose one of these situations and write a paragraph describing what is going on, what information is being synthesized, and what someone in that situation might conclude from the information being provided. For example: A person walks up to a counter in a fast-food restaurant. There are no other customers in the store, even though it is lunchtime. She sees that the food-preparation area looks dirty. She also sees that the prices are very high. The customer draws a conclusion and decides to go elsewhere for lunch.

- At home, have each student find an article in a newspaper or magazine about revitalizing a neighborhood or community. Tell them to read the article, bring it to class, and to prepare to summarize the article orally for the next class.

Use reading skills: Compare and contrast. Explain to students that *comparing* is telling how things are similar; *contrasting* is telling how things are different. Tell students that when they read they should look for comparisons and contrasts. Sorting our the similarities and differences can help students understand what they are reading about.

Use a graphic organizer. The relationships among the ideas in the text help the reader to see the way the text is organized. In this lesson, the Venn diagram visually organizes the dimensions so that the reader and the writer can see the dimensions on which to compare and contrast the old and new markets.

Write About It (PAGES 93–94)

Write a comparison. Have students read the directions on page 93. Be sure they understand that they will write a comparison of an old building or institution and the new one that replaced it. Students may choose a retail space, a school, a business, or a nationally known institution to write about.

Prewriting Remind students that buildings are renovated or replaced for many reasons. The changes may affect the building's appearance, character, and function. The changes may also affect how people feel about the building. Remind students to use the Venn diagram to help them compare and contrast the two institutions on the same dimensions. This will help them write their comparisons in an organized and logical manner.

Thinking Beyond Reading Have each student work with a partner or a small group to discuss the questions. The intent is for students to probe more deeply and to elaborate on the topic by addressing dimensions, ideas, or comparisons that did not arise when they were first thinking about the two buildings. Encourage them to add ideas to their Venn diagrams.

Write a draft. Have students write independently. Remind students to use the ideas in their Venn diagrams to organize the different elements of their responses. These will be the details in their paragraphs. Encourage students to use words that compare and contrast, such as *but, however,* and *on the contrary.* While drafting, students should not be concerned with spelling or punctuation. Encourage them to write their thoughts quickly and freely.

Revise and create a final draft. Remind students to use the Revising and Editing Checklist (Master 11) to guide them in revising their writing. Have students review each other's writing and give each other feedback on the parts of their paragraphs that are logical, clear, and interesting, and the parts that need revision. Have students give feedback on the structure of their partners' paragraphs.

When students have finished revising their writing, use the Writing Rubric (Master 10) to evaluate it. Be sure you review your response with each student so he or she understands the strengths and weaknesses of this piece of writing. Have students date the writing and put the completed pieces in their writing portfolios.

Building Fluency

Identify small sections from "Next Stop, Fulton Fish Market." Tell students that they will use echo reading to read these sections aloud. Put students into groups of two. Give them time to read a passage silently 2–3 times to encourage their best oral reading. Remind them to pay attention to words that cause them to stumble. Remind students to use punctuation and typographic cues to add expression to their reading. Tell them that the goal is to read the passage as fluently as if they were just speaking.

Spending and Saving

Lesson Overview: (PAGE 95)

Theme

Have students read the lesson title on page 95 and tell them that the title introduces the lesson theme, Consumerism and Money. Have students make personal connections, telling where and when they do their grocery shopping. Ask them whether they enjoy grocery shopping or view it as a chore.

Learning Objectives

Be sure students understand the outcome of each of the learning goals.

- *Learn about how to become a good grocery shopper.* Point out that this article is nonfiction and it gives practical information about how to save money and time when shopping for groceries.
- *Classify information you read.*
- *Master the key vocabulary used in the article.*
- *Write a description.*

Preteach the vocabulary. (PAGE 95)

Read the key vocabulary words and their definitions to students. Tell them that they will recognize all these words in the article.

- Distribute the Vocabulary Knowledge Rating Chart (Master 9) and have students individually rate each of the key vocabulary words.
- Preview particularly challenging words with students by listing each one on the board, modeling its use in a sentence, and having two or three students use the word in original sentences. Reframe student sentences that do not use the new words correctly.

You may wish to offer a mini-lesson on nouns as students read the respective parts of speech with the definitions of the vocabulary words. [See page 39 of this book for a mini-lesson on nouns. Use Master 1 or 2 to give students practice in recognizing nouns.]

Before You Read (PAGE 96)

Explain that good readers summarize as they read. This summarizing usually takes place in the reader's head, and it happens every few paragraphs or every page. The purpose of summarizing is to ensure that the reader understands the ideas he or she is reading. Readers who are not able to summarize effectively know they need to reread part of the text. Often readers write notes as they are reading. Encourage students to make notes in the margins of texts or on sticky notes as they are reading.

As students begin to write answers to the questions for each element on page 96, have them read the respective Think About Its.

Use what you know. Use the Think About It to elicit from students a discussion about their own experiences grocery shopping and how they feel about those experiences. Do students think that the sisters have a useful strategy for shopping efficiently?

Preview before you read. Have students read the title and say what they think the article will include. Then have them read the subheadings. How do they add to the information about the article. Do students have a good idea of what to expect they will learn in the article?

Reading the Article (PAGES 97–99)

Point out to students that they will read to learn ways to become a smarter shopper in the grocery store. It is a question to answer as they read. Jotting down notes in their notebooks or in the margins is a strategy that will keep them involved in the article.

Side-Column Vocabulary Remind students that the vocabulary words and phrases in the side column have been selected as important to the theme and content of the article. These words may be useful in the context of grocery shopping, but they are not necessarily part of everyday language.

Mid-Passage Questions Most of the answers to the questions are stated explicitly in the text. Students should be able to identify the sentences where they found their answers. Review students' written answers to assess whether they are getting meaning from the text. Students should be able to describe the layout of the typical grocery store. They should also be able to list some of the ideas they are willing to try when they shop.

After You Read (PAGES 100–102)

Build a robust vocabulary. Ask students to check their answers in the answer keys in their books.

Think about your reading. Ask students to check their answers in the answer keys in their books. Ask additional questions to enrich the discussion so that students will be better able to write about intelligent grocery shopping. Here are some possible questions:

- A good writer usually writes for a specific audience. The author includes certain information and omits other information depending on this intended audience. Who is the intended audience for this article? Have students provide evidence from the text to support their answers.

- How does *where* you choose to shop for groceries affect how much you spend and your overall experience?

Extend the reading. Here are some additional activities to expand students' understanding.

- With students working in pairs, have one partner read the text aloud, stopping at a logical breaking point. Then, have the listener summarize what the reader has read. The reader should feel free to disagree with or discuss the listener's summary.

- *For English Language Learners* Have students find examples of questions in the passage and related to the passage. Have students practice reading the questions aloud and then answering the questions in complete sentences, using much of the wording from the question. For example: "Does Kathy's experience sound familiar?" "Kathy's experience does not sound familiar because I enjoy grocery shopping." or "Which is the cheaper cake?" "The cheaper cake is Brand 1." Explain how questions are formed in English, with the subject and verb often inverted. Have pairs of students continue practicing by asking and answering additional questions.

- Guide students in a discussion about other types of stores and how they are organized. These could be major retailers such as Walmart or Target, or a department store or a local bodega. Have students classify information about a store into different categories of merchandise. Draw on the board a chart like the one on page 103 and have small groups of students discuss the organization of the store. Have the groups discuss and compare their charts. This activity will prepare students for the writing task to follow.

- At home, have students write notes after their next trips to the grocery store. Have students create Venn diagrams telling how their store is the same and different from the description in the article. During the next class, ask students to share their observations in small groups.

Use reading skills: Classify information. In an informational passage, the author often classifies similar ideas under a heading. In the article, the author uses subheadings such as "Save Time" and "Save Money" to help the reader. The process of classifying things takes related information or facts and makes it easier to understand and remember them. Have students talk about ways they classify things in their everyday lives.

Use a graphic organizer. In this lesson, the chart helps the writer organize the information from the article into related categories. The chart also helps the reader see the way the text is organized.

Write About It (PAGES 103–104)

Write a description.   Have students read the directions on page 103. Be sure they understand that they will write a description of another kind of store. The description will tell what the main departments or sections are in the store and what kinds of things are found in each section.

Prewriting   Students will use both the information from the passage and their own experience in stores. Point out that the graphic organizer breaks the task of organizing and describing the store into manageable parts. Tell students that thinking about each department or section and the kinds of things it includes will help them to organize their thinking. This will make it easier for them to write their descriptions in an organized manner.

Thinking Beyond Reading   Have each student work with a partner or a small group to discuss the questions. The intent is for students to probe more deeply and to elaborate on the topic by addressing issues that did not arise when they were first thinking about the store they will write about. Encourage them to add ideas to their charts.

Write a draft.   Have students write independently. Be sure students understand that all the sentences in their paragraphs must relate to the same main idea, in this case the particular store they are writing about and how it is organized. Remind students to use the ideas in their charts to organize their descriptions. While drafting, students should not be concerned with spelling or punctuation.

Encourage them to write their thoughts quickly and freely.

Revise and create a final draft.   Remind students to use the Revising and Editing Checklist (Master 11) to guide them in making revisions to their writing. Have students review each other's writing and give each other feedback on the parts of their descriptions that are logical, clear, and interesting, and the parts that need revision.

When students have finished revising their writing, use the Writing Rubric (Master 10) to evaluate it. Be sure you review your response with each student so he or she understands the strengths and weaknesses of this piece of writing. Have students date the writing and put the completed pieces in their writing portfolios.

Building Fluency

Identify small sections from "Be a Better Grocery Shopper." Tell students that they will use paired reading to read these sections aloud. Put students into groups of two. Give them time to read a passage silently 2–3 times to encourage their best oral reading. Partners take turns being the reader or listener. After the first reading, the listener does not provide feedback. After the second and third readings, the listener provides feedback to the reader. Remind students to pay attention to words that cause them to stumble and to read for the author's message. Their goal is to read the passage as fluently as if they were just speaking.

Grammar Mini-Lessons

LESSON 1: NOUNS

Learning Objectives
To define the term *noun*

To identify nouns

To generate nouns

Activate Prior Knowledge
Help students recall or find out what they know about *nouns*. Ask them to make verbal "wish lists" for their next birthdays or for a holiday. (Examples: *computer, clothes, toys for the children*) Write both the common and proper nouns they use on the board. Tell them that the words they used are called **nouns**.

Instruction
Tell the class that **nouns are the names of people, places, things, and ideas.** Then invite students to help you fill out a chart that you have drawn on the board.

Examples of Nouns			
People	**Places**	**Things**	**Ideas**

To begin, ask a volunteer to name a famous entertainer. (Examples: *Usher, Tom Cruise*) Then ask him to decide in which column he would write the name. (*people* column) Then, following the same procedure, ask volunteers to name the places in which the performer may be seen or heard and to name the equipment the performer might use. Finally, tell them to take a moment to think about and then name the qualities the entertainer is known for.

If students seem to be having difficulty with nouns as "ideas," tell them that *The names of ideas are not tangible; that is, they are not things that you can touch with your hands. But they are still nouns, just like names of people, places, and things.* Then, to help them generate nouns that are ideas, ask them try to complete a sentence, such as: *Usher is known for the _____ he shows during a performance.*

Examples of idea nouns might include the names of emotions (*joy* or *despair, anger* or *passion*) or character traits (*honesty, generosity* or *gentleness*).

When the chart is filled out, ask the class to write sentences, using two or more nouns in each one. Encourage them to try to include nouns that name ideas. (Example: *Usher's energy and originality makes his music special.*)

Noun Practice
For more student practice with nouns, distribute Master 1 or 2 in this Teacher's Guide.

LESSON 2: VERBS

Learning Objectives

To define the term *verb*

To identify verbs

To generate verbs

Activate Prior Knowledge

Help students recall or discover what they already know about verbs. Ask students to think about a favorite sport. Then invite volunteers to name actions associated with that sport. (Examples: *hit, kick, punch, drive, ride*) Write the verbs they use on the board. Tell students that each of those words is a **verb.**

Instruction

Write the word *walk* on the board. Direct the class to think of another word that means *to walk*. Then have volunteers say their words. (Examples: *amble, stroll, glide, march, roam*) Tell the class that these words are verbs. Write on the board: **Words that show action are called verbs.**

Then write the following three words on the board: *fry, blue, trout.* Ask students to name the word or words that show action. *(fry)* Underline that word.

Write on the board three or more columns of three words. Each column should include at least one verb. Have volunteers underline the verbs. Warn them that there might be more than one verb in a column. Examples:

fry	dive	bicycle	raised	trot	red	window
blue	artist	erase	clothing	piano	growl	subtract
trout	banana	draws	sat	lovely	atlas	clean

Ask students to create oral sentences using the underlined verbs. Challenge them to use as many verbs in one sentence as they can. (Examples: *We dive into the pool while they fry the fish. She draws and then erases her work. We raised the flag and then sat down to eat.*)

Point out to students that verbs can show time. Write on the board: *All day yesterday I* _____ *and* _____ . *All day tomorrow I will* _____ *and* _____ . Have students take turns completing the sentences by adding verbs.

Verb Practice

For more student practice with verbs, distribute Master 3 or 4 in this Teacher's Guide.

LESSON 3: ADJECTIVES

Learning Objectives
To define the term *adjective*
To identify adjectives
To generate adjectives

Activate Prior Knowledge
Help students recall or find out what they already know about *adjectives*. Ask volunteers to tell what is usually on their menus for a holiday family meal. Ask them to use two words— a noun and another word that describes it. Start by giving them examples of your own, such as *hot turkey, spicy stuffing,* and *brown gravy*. Write their responses on the board, underlining the adjectives as you do. Tell the class that these words—words that describe nouns—are called **adjectives.**

Instruction
Tell the class that **adjectives are words that describe nouns.** Elicit from students some common nouns. Start by asking them to name their favorite foods. Write two or three on the board in a column, as shown below.

Adjectives	Nouns
	pizza
	bagels
	donuts

Have a volunteer write a descriptive word (adjective) in the blank beside the noun. (Examples: *pizza—cold, cheesy, vegetarian; bagels—toasted, sliced, buttered; donuts—sweet, round, filled*) Then invite volunteers to create sentences using a noun and as many of the adjectives as they can think of. (Examples: *A hot, cheesy, vegetarian pizza is my favorite lunch. A toasted, sliced, buttered bagel is always my first choice. A sweet, round, filled donut is irresistible.*)

Tell students to write similar lists for descriptions of foods they hate. Ask: *What would you list under "Nouns?"* (Examples: *mushrooms, cauliflower, bread*) *What would you list under "Adjectives?"* (Examples: *brown, boiled, white*) Then have volunteers use their noun-adjective pairs in written sentences. Invite them to share their descriptions with the class.

Adjective Practice
For more student practice with adjectives, distribute Master 5 or 6 in this Teacher's Guide.

LESSON 4: ADVERBS

Learning Objectives

To define the term *adverb*

To identify adverbs

To generate adverbs

Activate Prior Knowledge

Help students recall or discover what they already know about *adverbs*. Invite the class to join in a round-robin activity. Ask each student to use one word to describe how they perform a particular task. Tell them to be sure their word answers the question "how?" For example, the task may be getting out of the house every morning to go to work. Each student would then take a turn describing how he or she accomplishes that task. (Examples: first student—*I open my eyes slowly;* second student—*I get up quickly;* third student—*I dress hurriedly.*] Write students' best and funniest adverbs on the board. Then tell students that the words they used to tell how are **adverbs.**

Instruction

Tell the class that **adverbs are words that describe verbs.** They answer the questions *How? When?* and *Where?* Draw the following chart on the board

Verb	ADVERBS		
	How?	When?	Where?

Elicit verbs from the class. Write the verbs in the left column. Then for each of the verbs ask students to provide the adverbs. Provide guidance by pointing to and asking the questions at the top of each column. (Example: *Work—How did he work? Slowly; When did he work? Today; Where did he work? There;* More examples: *eats—hungrily, always, outside*)

You may wish to have volunteers read aloud the examples they give to you in complete sentences. (Examples: *He woke slowly today there at home. Every morning inside her bedroom she dresses hurriedly. They always eat breakfast hungrily outside on the sunny deck.*)

Point out to students that adverbs may appear anywhere in a sentence. Often they are close to the verb, but sometimes they are not. Write examples on the board. As you describe where the verb and adverb are located, draw an arrow from the adverb to the verb. Examples:

I walked to work <u>quickly</u>.

<u>Quickly</u>, I walked to work.

I walked <u>quickly</u> to work.

Adverb Practice

For more student practice with adverbs, distribute Master 7 or 8 in this Teacher's Guide.

Master 1: Nouns 1

Student's Name _____

> **A noun is the name of a person, place, thing, or idea.**

Examples of nouns are listed in the chart below.

People	Places	Things	Ideas
nurse	clinic	bandage	skill
doctor	hospital	medicine	health

Finding Nouns: Underline the nouns in each sentence. HINT: There are 17 nouns.

1. The woman was a paramedic for ten years.

2. She saved a baby in a crash on the highway.

3. The family was driving home from the city.

4. The car skidded off the road and hit a tree.

5. The mother and father survived the accident.

6. The tree and the automobile did not.

Writing Nouns: Read the nouns. Write one noun in each sentence.

joy	peace	respect	beauty	laughter

7. Her _____ lies in her dark eyes and flowing hair.

8. It is a _____ to be in her company.

9. He earned our _____ the day of the fire.

10. I can still hear the sound of their _____.

11. They worked for _____ in the world.

Using Nouns: Write a noun to complete each sentence.

12. Quickly plan a menu for the _____.

13. Politely ask for the _____.

14. Neatly fold the _____.

15. Carefully slice the _____.

16. Quietly play the _____.

17. Finally turn off the _____.

Master 2: Nouns 2

Student's Name _____

A noun is the name of a person, place, thing, or idea.

Common nouns are the general names for people, places, things, or ideas.
Proper nouns are the names of very specific people, places, or things.

	Common Nouns	**Proper Nouns**
People	man	James Comer
Places	town	New Haven
Things	school	Yale University

Finding Nouns: Underline the proper nouns. Remember, many are composed of two or more words.
HINT: There are 9 proper nouns.

1. Marion Wright Edelman helped African Americans in Mississippi.

2. She works with the Robin Hood Foundation in New York.

3. A well known band, The Rolling Stones, raised money for it.

4. She is famous for her work with the Children's Defense Fund.

5. She was influenced by civil rights leader A. Philip Randolph.

6. Her father, Reverend Arthur Wright, is a preacher.

Writing Nouns: Write the common nouns in each sentence.

7. His first school is located in Philadelphia. _____

8. He was on television and won an Emmy. _____

9. Bill is an outstanding American actor. _____

10. He created the funny show, "Fat Albert." _____

11. There he wrote about his own childhood. _____

12. He played a doctor on "The Cosby Show." _____

13. The new cartoon, "Little Bill," is quite famous. _____

Using Nouns: Write a proper noun for each common noun.

14. actor _____

15. singer _____

16. river _____

17. city _____

18. holiday _____

19. state _____

Master 3: Verbs 1

Student's Name _____

A verb is a word that shows action.

The underlined words are verbs. They show action.

    She <u>hammers</u> nails.   They <u>hang</u> windows.   You <u>punch</u> rivets.
    He <u>turns</u> screws.   It <u>spreads</u> cement.   We <u>saw</u> wood.

Finding Verbs: Circle the verb in each sentence. HINT: Two sentences have more than one verb.

1. People sometimes waste useful materials.

2. Today we recycle paper, glass, and cans.

3. They gather the bottles on the ground in the park.

4. People sort the bottles by their colors.

5. Workers collect the bags in the morning.

6. Machines crush the glass and melt it.

7. Some companies use it in pavement for roads.

8. We save money and create more jobs.

Writing Verbs: Write the verb in each sentence.

9. Sears Roebuck needed more space. _____

10. They built the Sears Tower in Chicago. _____

11. Construction started in August 1970. _____

12. Today the Sears Tower stands among the world's tallest buildings. _____

13. TV antennas make it even higher. _____

Using Verbs: For each verb, write another verb with the opposite meaning.

Example: laugh ___cry_____

14. spend _____   19. frown _____

15. accept _____   20. harm _____

16. open _____   21. give _____

17. finish _____   22. forget _____

18. follow _____   23. stay _____

Master 4: Verbs 2   Student's Name _____

A verb is a word that shows action.

The underlined words are verbs.

Verbs	**Time of Action**
It <u>snows</u> in the mountains.	present
Hail <u>tumbled</u> from the sky.	past
It <u>will melt</u> soon enough.	future

Finding Verbs: Underline the verb in each sentence. Circle the time it shows.

1. John Forbes creates parks and museums.   present   past
2. Atlanta thanks him for his work.   future   present
3. Bankers supported his plan for a nature preserve.   past   present
4. He saved it from the rush of cars and trucks.   past   present
5. It will contain oak, walnut, and elm trees.   present   future
6. The news called him a "Johnny Appleseed."   past   future

Writing Verbs: Write the verb in each sentence.

7. The man trained as a Marine. _____
8. He raises the flag in a famous photo. _____
9. Hayes enlisted early in the war. _____
10. He will sail on the ocean with other troops. _____
11. He soon joined the battle for a hill in Japan. _____
12. He and several others became national heroes. _____
13. He will return home a more mature person. _____

Using Verbs: Underline the verbs. Then write each verb to show a different time.

Example: An old cow <u>chews</u> her cud. ___will chew___

14. A goose waddles on the lawn. _____
15. A hog nuzzles the ground. _____
16. A grey wolf gnaws on a bone. _____
17. A polar bear dozes on the ice. _____
18. A monkey howls in the trees. _____
19. A child laughs in delight. _____

Master 5: Adjectives 1

Student's Name

An adjective is a word that describes a noun.

The adjectives in the sentences below are underlined.

I have <u>five</u> brothers.
Let's have a <u>pleasant</u> meal.
Go find the <u>green</u> tablecloth.

Finding Adjectives: The first column is a list of nouns. Draw a line to connect each one to an adjective. The first one is done for you.

NOUNS   **ADJECTIVES**

1. peppers   • crunchy
2. chicken   • large
3. meatballs   • sweet
4. rice   • juicy
5. peach   • spicy
6. carrots   • brown

Writing Adjectives: Write the adjective that describes the underlined noun in each sentence.

7. The wise <u>woman</u> was speaking to us. _____

8. The old <u>forests</u> are disappearing. _____

9. The rich <u>soil</u> will wash away. _____

10. Tell ten <u>people</u> to plant trees. _____

11. Sit with me under the shady <u>leaves</u>. _____

12. Do you want fresh <u>water</u> to drink? _____

13. Give the animals a cool <u>place</u> to live. _____

Using Adjectives: Write an adjective to describe each noun.

14. _____ lettuce   18. _____ pickles

15. _____ burgers   19. _____ tomatoes

16. _____ buns   20. _____ cheese

17. _____ ketchup   21. _____ bacon

Master 6: Adjectives 2

Student's Name _____

An adjective is a word that describes a noun.

The adjectives in the sentences below are underlined.

The <u>winding</u> road leads to a <u>small</u> town.
An <u>old</u> sedan stops at a <u>red</u> light.
<u>Two</u> people open the <u>rusty</u> doors.

Finding Adjectives: The nouns in each sentence are underlined. Circle the adjectives that describe them.

1. A massive <u>volcano</u> is now only a large <u>crater</u>.

2. Curious <u>visitors</u> go to see it every <u>year</u>.

3. There they find pure <u>waters</u> and stunning <u>colors</u>.

4. Steep <u>cliffs</u> surround the beautiful <u>place</u>.

5. Deep <u>snows</u> melt and fill the ancient <u>basin</u>.

6. It is the deepest <u>lake</u> in this huge <u>country</u>.

Writing Adjectives: Write the two adjectives in each sentence.

7. The small world orbits a blue planet. _____

8. A bright circle lights the dark sky. _____

9. The same side always faces the good Earth. _____

10. The other part is always pitch black. _____

11. The dry surface is covered with fine dust. _____

12. A new moon occurs every 30 days or so. _____

Using Adjectives: Write an adjective to complete each sentence.

13. Sit by the _____ window.

14. Breathe in the _____ air.

15. Look at the _____ sky.

16. Count the _____ lights.

17. Wish on the _____ star.

Master 7: Adverbs 1

Student's Name

> **An adverb is a word that describes a verb.**

The underlined words are adverbs. They tell *how, when,* and *where.*

Winter weather arrived <u>suddenly</u>. (arrived *how?*)

We shoveled snow <u>today</u>. (shoveled *when?*)

Over nine inches fell <u>here</u>. (fell *where?*)

Finding Adverbs: Verbs are underlined in each sentence. Circle the adverbs that describe them. HINT: Remember that adverbs do not have to be immediately before or after the verb.

1. In the winter, the geese <u>fly</u> there from Canada.

2. Canada geese often <u>nest</u> on small islands.

3. The goose <u>chooses</u> her nest site carefully.

4. She quickly <u>gathers</u> twigs, grass, and moss.

5. She lays eggs and then <u>surrounds</u> them with feathers.

6. The mating pairs usually <u>stay</u> together for life.

7. <u>Find</u> them anywhere in the northern regions.

Writing Adverbs: Write the adverbs you circled in the correct column.

How?	When?	Where?
8.	10.	13.
9.	11.	14.
	12.	

Using Adverbs: Complete each sentence with an adverb from the box.

always	carefully	silently	perfectly	slowly

15. Walk _____ in the woods.

16. Lift your camera _____.

17. Focus the lens _____.

18. Capture the image _____.

Master 8: Adverbs 2

Student's Name _____

An adverb is a word that describes a verb.

These words are adverbs. They tell how, when, and where.

How?   gently, softly, wildly
When?   now, usually, lately
Where? outside, nearby, there

Finding Adverbs: The verbs are underlined. Circle each adverb that describes a verb.

1. A grey cat once <u>visited</u> an old man.

2. It eagerly <u>jumped</u> onto his lap in the morning.

3. The man <u>brushed</u> the cat well for an hour.

4. It suddenly <u>leaped</u> through the open window.

5. He <u>looked</u> for it everywhere in the city.

6. Meanwhile he <u>adopted</u> an old stray tabby.

7. The two of them <u>live</u> in one room happily.

Writing Adverbs: Write the adverb from each sentence.

8. My cat opens cabinet doors often. _____

9. Then it cries in the dark for help. _____

10. Cats easily identify the odor of catnip. _____

11. Some cats react badly to anything strange. _____

12. They may protest noisily or hide for days. _____

Using Adverbs: Write an adverb to complete each sentence. Try to include adverbs that tell *when* and *where*, as well as *how*.

13. Bathe it _____.

14. Brush it _____.

15. Feed it _____.

16. Pet it _____.

17. Run with it _____.

18. Play with it _____.

19. Train it _____.

20. Sit with it _____.

Master 9: Vocabulary Knowledge Rating Chart   Student's Name

Vocabulary Word	1	2	3	4	5
		I know this word. I can explain its meaning and use it when I speak and write.	I think I know this word. It has something to do with _____.	I've seen or heard this word, but I'm not sure what it means.	I don't know this word. I need to learn it.

Master 10: Writing Rubric

Student's Name _____

	Focus	Organization	Voice	Conventions
4	Ideas are on the topic and interesting.	There is a clearly presented main idea with supporting details, facts, and/or opinions. The writing flows very well.	The writer speaks to the audience clearly. Word choice is varied, and the words were chosen because they are the very best words for getting the point across.	Contains few, if any, errors in grammar, punctuation, capitalization, and/or spelling. Any errors that do occur do not get in the way of the reader's understanding.
3	Ideas are on the topic.	There is a main idea with supporting details, facts, and/or opinions. The writing flows.	The writer speaks to the audience. Word choice is varied and gets the point across.	Contains some errors in grammar, punctuation, capitalization, and/or spelling. These errors do not get in the way of the reader's understanding.
2	Ideas may be a bit off of the topic.	Although there is a main idea and/or details, the writing is sometimes difficult to follow.	The writer shows some understanding of the audience. Words are repeated too often and/or misused.	Contains several errors in grammar, punctuation, capitalization, and/or spelling. These errors may get in the way of the reader's understanding of the writing.
1	Ideas are not on the topic.	It is difficult for the reader to follow the writer's arguments or explanations.	The writer does not speak to the audience. Words are repeated too often and/or misused.	Contains serious errors in grammar, punctuation, capitalization, and/or spelling. These errors make the writing very difficult for the reader to understand.

Master 11: Revising and Editing Checklist   Student's Name

When you **revise,** you add to or take away from your writing to make it clearer and more understandable. It always helps to read your work to a partner so that you can make sure it is well organized, includes enough details, and makes sense.

When you **edit,** look at the specific words you have chosen. Are they the best words? Check your work for proper spelling, punctuation, and usage. Make sure that you have not left out or repeated a word. Have you used correct grammar?

Always revise before you edit. You don't want to spend time editing something you may not include in your revision.

Revising

_____ I read the writing to myself to see if it made sense.

_____ I read the writing to a partner to see if it made sense.

_____ My writing stays on the topic.

_____ My paragraph has a topic sentence and includes supporting details.

_____ My writing is logical and well organized.

_____ The writing is interesting.

_____ I used enough information and examples to make my point.

_____ My ending ties up the writing.

Editing

_____ Each of my sentences ends with a period (.), a question mark (?), or an exclamation point (!).

_____ My subjects and verbs agree.

_____ I have used commas correctly.

_____ Each of my sentences begins with a capital letter.

_____ I have used quotation marks correctly.

_____ My paragraph is indented.

_____ I chose my words carefully so that the reader can visualize just what I'm talking about.

_____ I inserted words that add interest to my writing.

_____ I inserted words that were missing.

_____ I deleted extra words that I didn't need.

_____ I circled words that I think may be incorrectly spelled. I used additional resources to check the spelling of those words.

_____ I gave my edited draft to a partner to check.

Master 12: Editor's Marks   Student's Name

Use these marks when editing a paper. Make sure you understand what the marks mean when a teacher or partner uses them on your paper.

Editing Marks		
≡	Changes a lowercase letter to an uppercase letter.	I visited kiwanis park with my cousins. ≡ ≡
/	Changes an uppercase letter to a lowercase letter.	Maria brought her Ð̸og.
∧	Adds a word or punctuation mark.	We biked ∧ the park. *to*
ℓ	Deletes a word or punctuation mark.	We ran around the the playground.
▭	Indicates incorrect word choice.	We had a lot of fun their. *there*
◯	Indicates a misspelled word.	We plan to go agin next weekend. *again*

Answers to Masters 1–8

MASTER 1: NOUNS 1

1. woman, paramedic, years
2. baby, crash, highway
3. family, home, city
4. car, road, tree
5. mother, father, accident
6. tree, automobile
7. beauty
8. joy
9. respect
10. laughter
11. peace
12.–18. Answers will vary.

MASTER 2: NOUNS 2

1. Marion Wright Edelman, African Americans, Mississippi
2. Robin Hood Foundation, New York
3. The Rolling Stones
4. Children's Defense Fund
5. A. Philip Randolph
6. Reverend Arthur Wright
7. school
8. television
9. actor
10. show
11. childhood
12. doctor
13. cartoon
14.–19. Answers will vary.

MASTER 3: VERBS 1

1. waste
2. recycle
3. gather
4. sort
5. collect
6. crush, melt
7. use
8. save, create
9. needed
10. built
11. started
12. stands
13. make
14.–23. Answers will vary. Possible answers:
14. save
15. reject
16. close
17. start
18. lead
19. smile
20. help
21. take
22. remember
23. leave

MASTER 4: VERBS 2

1. creates, present
2. thanks, present
3. supported, past
4. saved, past
5. will contain, future
6. called, past
7. trained
8. raises
9. enlisted
10. will sail
11. joined
12. became
13. will return
14. waddles; waddled or will waddle
15. nuzzles; nuzzled or will nuzzle
16. gnaws; gnawed or will gnaw
17. dozes; dozed or will doze
18. howls; howled or will howl
19. laughs; laughed or will laugh

MASTER 5: ADJECTIVES 1

1.–6. Answers will vary.
Possible answers:
1. sweet
2. large
3. spicy
4. brown
5. juicy
6. crunchy
7. wise
8. old
9. rich
10. ten
11. shady
12. fresh
13. cool
14.–21. Answers will vary.

MASTER 6: ADJECTIVES 2

1. massive, large
2. Curious, every
3. pure, stunning
4. Steep, beautiful
5. Deep, ancient
6. deepest, huge
7. small, blue
8. bright, dark
9. same, good
10. other, pitch
11. dry, fine
12. new, 30
13.–17. Answers will vary.

MASTER 7: ADVERBS 1

1. there
2. often
3. carefully
4. quickly
5. then
6. usually
7. anywhere
8. carefully
9. quickly
10. often
11. then
12. usually
13. there
14. anywhere
15.–18. Answers will vary. Possible answers:
15. silently
16. slowly
17. carefully
18. perfectly

MASTER 8: ADVERBS 2

1. once
2. eagerly
3. well
4. suddenly
5. everywhere
6. Meanwhile
7. happily
8. often
9. Then
10. easily
11. badly
12. noisily
13.–20. Answers will vary.

$12.00   7/21/15

LONGWOOD PUBLIC LIBRARY
800 Middle Country Road
Middle Island, NY 11953
(631) 924-6400
longwoodlibrary.org

LIBRARY HOURS

Monday-Friday	9:30 a.m. - 9:00 p.m.
Saturday	9:30 a.m. - 5:00 p.m.
Sunday (Sept-June)	1:00 p.m. - 5:00 p.m.